VISUAL RESEARCH METHODS IN DESIGN

Henry Sanoff

Department of Architecture
School of Design
North Carolina State University

VNR Van Nostrand Reinhold
_____ New York

Copyright © 1991 by Van Nostrand Reinhold

Library of Congress Catalog Number: 90–37290
ISBN 0-442-23827-4

Printed in the United States of America

Van Nostrand Reinhold
115 Fifth Avenue
New York, New York 10003

Chapman and Hall
2–6 Boundary Row
London, SE1 8HN, England

Thomas Nelson, Australia
102 Dodds Street
South Melbourne 3205, Victoria Australia

Nelson Canada
1120 Birchmount Road
Scarborough, Ontario M1K 5G4, Canada

16 15 14 13 12 11 10 9 8 7 6 5 4 3 2 1

Library of Congress Cataloging-in-Publication Data

Sanoff, Henry.
   Visual research methods in design/by Henry Sanoff.
     p. cm.
   Includes bibliographical references and index.
   ISBN 0-442-23827-4
   1. Architectural design—Research. 2. Signs and symbols in architecture. 3. Architecture—Environmental aspects. I. Title.
NA2750.S25 1991
720'.28—dc20
                                         90-37290
                                           CIP

to Joan, Ari and Zöe

Contents

Preface

This book is about applications and issues related to the visual environment. The content pertains to the understanding of human behavior in the environment by recording behavior and actions or by direct interaction with people. It is about research and planning methods that primarily stress the visual features of the physical environment.

We carry with us images that influence our expectations, our actions, and our ways of seeing. While environment-behavior research has not totally ignored these aspects of our experience, little has been done to investigate meanings. In fact, most of the literature about environmental imagery and meaning is in verbal form, with occasional supportive illustrations.

Traditionally, environmental research has relied on verbal descriptions and perceptions of the physical environment, virtually ignoring the important visual component. Visual imagery has been given very little attention in environment-behavior research. Designers also have overlooked the application of social science techniques for acquiring visual information. So, too, social scientists, who have focused on the characteristics of a group of people living in a particular place, often ignore the visual surrounds. By expanding the visual information base, we can understand more about the form, action, and interpretations given to environmental settings. Our understanding of social activity can be greatly enhanced by attention to the inside and outside appearance of the environment. Understanding and producing images, and questioning what they mean, is the central theme of this book.

Various strategies have been explored that can expand our recorded visual information base. Diagramming, photo-interviewing, photo-sorting, mapping, notation, simulation, videotaping, and CADD suggest the range of media and methods available for expanding our comprehension of our everyday visual environment. A focus on visual information as a medium for communication can expand the dialogue between researchers and respondents, between researchers and designers, and between designers and clients.

Introduction

There appears to be a growing dissatisfaction with the visual environment of the past few decades, in contrast to the positive feelings evoked by its historical predecessors. This inability to effectively embrace issues of visual quality can be traced to many factors, least of which is the planning and design process. The tradition of criticism in the design fields, too, has contributed to superficial reactions of highly subjective judgments about the quality of the environment. Consequently, criticism has very little value for design professionals because it fails to explain the reasons for those subjective judgments. As a result, design professionals rely upon their intuition for decisions about visual quality. Research, however, indicates that professionals differ from the public in their environmental preferences (Canter, 1969; Groat, 1982; Hershberger and Cass, 1974). While some designers have little interest in public values, many professionals seek to produce user-sensitive environments. Therefore, inquiry into the application of research findings to design and planning can have a positive impact on improving the quality of the environment.

Integrating design research and practice can be viewed as a new strategy for achieving a productive dialogue about the visual environment. The notion stems, in part, from Lewin's (1946) concept of action research, a model that integrates theory and practice. This approach no longer calls for more applied research, nor for a form of research findings usable by practitioners. This new attitude does not deny the need for basic research, but has substantial implications for a new outlook on the practice of architecture and planning.

The rationale for a new professional outlook is not necessarily unique to the design field, but to the ubiquitous gulf between academics and professionals, between theoreticians and practitioners, or between researchers and designers, in all fields. While there have been valiant efforts by many disciplines to "bridge the gap," there still remains a gulf between the fund of available visual information and the application of this knowledge. In a similar way, conventional architectural practice usually undervalues the expertise of the users and denies their involvement in decision making. Quite often, design professionals and the public do not share the same aesthetic values. Designers differ from the public in their reactions to the environment. This factor has significance for the development of aesthetic controls and public policy, since community decisions about aesthetic regulations often requires strong support for aesthetic judgments.

Although visual input in the design process is inadequate, user-relevant decisions about their visual environment have increasingly become a requirement in finding community acceptance. People who use the environment, who are the traditional subjects of research, can become active participants in the research, and, consequently, in changing the environment. This idea is predicated on the belief that people who use the environment have an expertise equal to, but different from, the expertise of the design professional. User involvement, then, becomes a central component of the research approach. Users can evaluate research results and subsequently develop recommendations about how to address environmental problems.

This action approach offers design professionals, who are concerned with users' visual comprehension of the environment, a new set of social science tools. These new tools provide designers not only with a deeper understanding of people's perception of the environment, but also an opportunity for engaging in an effective dialogue with people who use the environment. This is in contrast to the use of more casual methods of inquiry, which typically reveal what is already obvious, or traditional social science approaches, which tend to verbally describe the visual environment.

There are many benefits accruing from an integrative approach for the community, the users, and the designer. First, from the social point of view, integrating research and participation can result in a greater meeting of people's visual needs and an increasingly effective utilization of resources at the disposal of a particular community (Cashden, Fahle, Francis, Schwartz, and Stein, 1978). Second, to the user group, it represents an increased sense of having influenced the design decision-making process and an increased awareness of the consequences of decisions made. Third, to the design professional, it provides more relevant and up-to-date information than was possible before.

If we are concerned with improving the quality of the physical world around us, it is evident that there needs to be an increased awareness of the impact of the visual environment on people's everyday lives. This renewed awareness can be brought about in many ways. One approach seeks to integrate research into the design process as an integral element of information gathering. The benefit of this approach is that future decisions about visual quality can become the product of informed designers' intuition.

The enhancement of environmental knowledge has been an issue for more than a decade, constituting the main idea behind all environmental education trends. There is no question of its value in building the sense of citizenship essential for the care and improvement of the world we live in.

A large portion of the work in the field has dealt with the built environment. Yet, more emphasis has been placed on information about its physical character than on the more abstract aspect of the relationship between people and their physical surroundings. This field of environmental study is still new, with no established research conclusions and some contradictions. But the increase in the amount of inquiry, and the spectrum of interested researchers and practitioners, acknowledge this "complex, systematic, ecological interaction" (Rapoport, 1971).

This book deals with that relationship, with the intent of increasing the awareness of nonverbal environmental messages which are important to our psychological well-being in a place. It raises questions and issues which, while constantly affecting our relationship with the environment, sometimes remain unnoticed during our daily experience. In short, this work is an attempt to bring forward, through a variety of methods, psychological effects that the physical world exerts upon us.

One might question the need for awareness of these effects. It is in the physical world itself, the world that we create and change according to our needs and values, that we find reasons.

Urban environments, for instance, especially those of large cities, are constantly changing and growing, often indiscriminately. Buildings are demolished to give place to new ones, and neighborhoods are modified to create more space for cars. Decisions are made under the guise of progress, to facilitate their acceptance by those who do not have a say in the decision-making process.

However, such changes have many more effects than we might realize. When buildings are demolished and neighborhoods modified, familiar environments become unfamiliar, altering our feelings of comfort and safety. We lose the ability to orient ourselves and spend more time determining where we are in relation to where we want to go. More significantly, we cease to identify with places and things that surround us because their formerly unique characteristics have been homogenized for the sake of practicality and economics. At the extreme, large-scale urban projects are so interjected into existing cultural and physical situations that marked and distressing forms of antisocial behavior result. The necessary destruction of the Pruitt-Igoe complex in St. Louis is still one of the most convincing examples of environmental psychosis that we have.

In short, continuous and indiscriminate changes contribute to the creation of environments at least lacking the character of their local makers and users, and often introduce inappropriate and destructive forces. As evidence of contemporary dissatisfaction with urban environments in particular increases, the need for understanding and knowledgeably modulating the interaction of people and place becomes more critical. Variety and change, nonetheless, are necessary ingredients of a pleasurable, memorable, and healthy environment. Becoming aware of perceived environmental effects is a necessary first step in striking the delicate balance between familiarity and monotony and boredom, and between variety and confusion and disorientation. With understanding of how physical surroundings affect us psychologically, we can become more aware of our effects on them, and on ourselves, when we allow them to be changed. We will then start to realize the importance of our concern for our surroundings, and eventually work toward the improvement of their quality.

We may think twice before deciding how to remodel an old building, taking care that it remains familiar to us and to other members of our community. Or we may design the public spaces of our towns to be pleasant environments in which even outsiders feel comfortable and safe. Awareness of our psychological relationship with the built environment should help us to recognize problems and work for their solution. Ultimately, it should make us better citizens in arousing our sense of responsibility for the world that surrounds us, deliberately making some decisions and accepting others.

Nonverbal environmental messages are part of all of our experiences, and are conveyed in many parts of our immediate surroundings. For the purposes of this work, they have been categorized under four major concepts—identity, orientation, meaning, and territoriality. Explained separately for clarity, they maintain a close relationship to one another. Further, places in the environment have been identified where those messages are often "read." Such places are described in scenarios where sequences of activities take place, and related messages and concepts are studied. These are entrances, buildings, inside buildings, and pathways.

Some of the places that stand out visually in the environment are familiar to us, either because they have been part of our everyday experiences, or because they are similar to places we have experienced in the past. Through learning, these are the places that "tell" us about people and their activities, and evoke either good or bad feelings reflecting our present sensations and associations we make with our past.

A place has meaning to us as individuals when it relates to, and has in fact become the setting for, events of our personal life. It can be a secret location in the yard where we used to hide to be alone with our thoughts, the place where we met a best friend for the first time, or any of the places whose meaning only we can understand.

Some meanings are shared by a group or even by a whole community, when they relate to the events of its communal life. The school we attended during childhood, for instance, has meaning to all of our former peers; and the very word *hometown* is meaningful to everyone who grew up there. On a more abstract level, the concept of meaning allows us to recognize the nature and purpose of places in the environment because of their resemblance to others of the type. Recognition and deliberate repetition of meaningful elements provide a culture with a powerful mechanism for self-proclamation and stability.

Familiarity with places through direct experience depends upon how many times we visit them, and how long each visit lasts. Through increasing involvement we "learn" a place, and it eventually becomes the area where we feel most comfortable and safe. Familiarity through association with past experiences does not imply a continuing deep involvement, but it does make us more understanding and responsive. In any case, to be familiar with a place is to share identity with it.

The ability to identify features in our environment is to recognize visual elements that stand out in the landscape by their size, height, color, or any other aspect that contrasts with the surroundings. It is to see characteristic elements in a background, which can range from a door in the wall, to a building in the streetscape, a park in the neighborhood, and so on. The ability to identify parts of the environment allows us to recognize the familiar as well as to appreciate the new.

The identification of elements in the landscape is extremely important to our sense of orientation within the environment. Only after recognizing a specific point or location can we establish its spatial relationship with ourselves, thus knowing where we are and how we should move (Canter, 1983).

The intention of this book is to identify visual methods for explaining the physical environment in a way that will enable researchers and designers to find a common mode of communication. Many of the techniques traditionally used by researchers have application potential for designers. Similarly, approaches used by designers equally lend themselves to a more systematic use by researchers.

Each section of the book discusses a different method for describing and communicating features of the visual environment. Included are a variety of studies conducted by the author, and others that focus on how the environment communicates messages to the viewer, how to observe and document behavior in the enveloping environment, how to portray two- and three-dimensional environments, and finally, how these methods are applied by architects and planners.

ACKNOWLEDGMENT

Support for the literature search was provided by the Center for Design Research and Service, School of Design, North Carolina State University. A special note of thanks is also due to my research assistant, Diane H. Filipowicz, who made a significant contribution to the development of this project.

1

ENVIRONMENTAL MEASUREMENT

The environment in which we live and work includes both a social and a physical component. Yet, because of the nature of professional study, there appears to be an arbitrary division between the two. There are the architects who shape the structure of the physical environment to make "places." And there are social scientists who have focused on the characteristics of a group of people living in a particular "place." Ostrander (1974) describes the problem as "the visual-semantic communication gap." It is his contention that social scientists are analytical thinkers, separating things into parts and subsequently looking for relationships between these parts. Designers, on the other hand, combine the parts into a unified whole. Recently, however, there has emerged an awareness of the interaction between the two components. However, one of the problems of integrating the two dimensions stems from the problems in social science practice, which attempts to investigate people's perceptions of the environment without structuring those perceptions. But, in fact, quite often the questions used in an interview organize and influence the perceptions of those interviewed.

Different approaches have been used to resolve this dilemma. One approach is to accompany residents on a community walk, asking particular questions about the environment. A direct comparison in a study by Lowenthal and Riel (1972) indicated that representational systems for directly experienced places and for images of places were similar. Another approach is to have people describe their environment by drawing maps of where they live (Gould & White, 1974). The assumption behind these studies is that cognitive maps of the environment are acquired predominantly through direct experience. Knowledge is gained about the perceptual characteristics of places by walking from one place to another (Gärling & Golledge, 1989). Yet another approach has been through interviews using photographs of the environment to generate insights about resident familiarity (Greenbie, 1976) and preferences (Zube et al., 1975; Sanoff, 1970a). Generally, the results of studies of images appear to be similar to those obtained in studies of direct place experiences (for example, Ward & Russell, 1981). However, even though the methods used to represent a place may be the same, a particular place may not be perceived exactly as it has been remembered. Changing conditions from one occasion to another may cause forgetting to occur (Mainardi-Peron, Baroni, Job, & Salmaso, 1985). Using photographic images as a basis for interviewing lies somewhere between use of verbal questions and conducting community walks.

Questionnaires and interviews can draw on a wide range of visual media. Photographs contain a vast resource of information and are often less ambiguous than words. There are certain situations where photographic images are appropriate for interviewing and others where drawings or models would be appropriate. There are always questions of reliability, such as the relationship between a visual image and the phenomenon it was intended to record, or people's ability to read the images. These questions of technique will continue to plague researchers, but first there must be recognition of the significance of visual images, while questions about their meanings continue to be raised.

Images used to represent the environment consider certain visual features as sources of aesthetic value. These values, such as visual quality, are not only a natural resource, but often the basis for public policy initiatives. The importance of visual quality has been recognized by such initiatives as the National Environmental Policy Act (1969) and the Coastal Zone Management Act (1972), as well as architectural review boards, downtown improvement associations, and other organizations. Furthermore, the United States Supreme Court has cited aesthetic criteria alone as an adequate basis for development (Pearlman, 1988). Therefore, discussions of environmental quality, in this context, refer to visual-aesthetic quality in the physical environment. This includes the scenic quality of the urban environment and scenic landscapes in the non-urban environment.

Appraisal measures the interaction between the human observer and the visual environment. Observer-based assessments of environmental quality consist of preferential judgments and comparative appraisals (Craik & Zube, 1976). Preferential judgments represent subjective reactions to specific environments, while comparative appraisals judge the quality of specific environments against a standard of comparison (Craik & McKechnie, 1974).

The environment can be represented by different modes. Although verbal descriptions have been used to represent the environment, direct and indirect methods decrease the possibility for misrepresentation. One method is to present the relevant features of the environment directly to observers. Direct representations may be made in the natural setting, thus minimizing opportunities for error when environments are represented by simulations. The major problem is the difficulty in controlling extraneous factors that may affect the observer's judgment.

Indirect representations are used most often and vary widely with the features of the environment being studied. Graphic representations are used where visually perceived properties of the environment are being assessed.

Specific measures should be taken to ensure unbiased representation using indirect methods. Since observers' judgments will be based on their interpretations of the represented environment, the quality of the representation is critical. The represented environment should reflect the properties and characteristics of the actual environment to be assessed. Comparative appraisals of visual displays are particularly sensitive to the slightest variation in the characteristics they represent. For example, Figures 1-1A and 1B are photographs of different buildings serving the same purposes. In Figure 1A, the building is placed in a landscaped setting, while in Figure 1B, the setting is barren. Comparative judgments of the buildings will undoubtedly be biased by the influence of the setting on the overall appearance of the buildings.

One of the unresolved problems of visual research is the measurement of properties chosen for study. Typically, this research has "completely sidestepped this problem, by the expedient of selecting environmental sites, views, structures, paths, or verbally designated locales or regions, without any attempt to assess these with respect to specific variables of the stimulus" (Wohlwill, 1976). Environmental images are usually presented, in the form of photographs or slides, to subjects who rate them on a large number of rating scales. The outcome of such studies tends to be descriptive of the way people respond verbally to environmental images, without necessarily establishing relationships among physical variables. These relationships need to be identified and assessed, and sometimes isolated, independently of the evaluative responses made to them.

Objective measures of physical characteristics of the environment that are related to human factors are typically temperature, noise level, and, in the visual area, brightness. The variables most relevant for studying the visual environment tend to be qualitative. Often, the factors measured, such as complexity, tend to be very abstract. Examples of more concrete features of the environment are provided in the landscape-feature checklist employed in the Connecticut River Valley study of Zube (Zube, Pitt, & Anderson, 1974). Shafer (1969) described natural landscape configurations with a total of forty-six variables,

Figure 1-1a: Building a landscaped setting (Photo: Lucien Kroll).

Figure 1-1b: Building in a barren setting (Photo: Lucien Kroll).

which included combinations of zones (such as sky, vegetation, lake, and so on) in order to obtain groupings of physical factors to predict preference judgments.

Although most physical methods involve a certain degree of personal judgment, there are situations that require the use of human judges to assess features of the visual environment. To be effective the scales should refer to the attributes of the environment rather than to subjective experiences. Landscape rating scales developed by Craik (1972) and landscape quality ratings used by Zube (Zube, Pitt & Anderson, 1974) reflect the subjective approach with reliable results. Zube's Scenic Quality scale (1976) uses landscape dimensions, such as topographic texture, land use diversity, percentage of tree cover, and so forth, which have a clear environmental referrent compared to scales such as pleasant–unpleasant, or ugly–beautiful, which refer to the individual's affective response.

Image selection, too, is in need of considerable clarification. Image sampling, as opposed to sampling of subjects, has largely been ignored. This was primarily a result of a history of research based on laboratory experimentation where the image or stimulus was constructed to represent the variables to be manipulated. As a result, the issue of sampling has rarely arisen. Representative sampling of environments is problematic because it is intended to arrive at a set of images that accurately correspond to attributes of the larger whole. Generalizability of results depends on successful sampling of images or stimuli. Brunswik (1956) argued for sampling of the environment in order to capture the range of conditions that typically confront the observer. Representative sampling was rejected by Hochberg (1966), who preferred the systematic variation of stimuli that are experienced in the environment. Wohwill (1976) suggested identifying the major variables in specific locales, necessitating prior investigation of sites included in the sample to establish environmental variables.

MULTIPLE SORTING

A number of different studies have demonstrated the potential of multiple sorting in establishing people's ratings of a variety of elements and situations (Canter, Brown, & Groat, 1985). Rather than suggesting a set of bipolar dichotomies or numerical weightings which can be applied to tested items, the technique allows people to sort items freely, according to their own criteria, into as many categories as they can describe. This type of sorting establishes not only the actual distribution of elements, but also reveals personal categorization schemes and related meanings and associations. Results may be more valid in determining human responses than those obtained when the tester supplies categories and values, and can suggest the important issues and aspects of the research itself.

The technique is simple, and can be carried out by giving subjects a set of elements and general instructions, such as those below. The italics indicate where instructions are likely to change with different research questions and procedures.

> We are conducting a study of people's thoughts and feelings about *landscapes*. So we are asking a number of people *chosen at random* to look at the following pictures and sort them into groups in such a way that all the pictures in a group are *similar to each other* in some way and different from those in other groups. You can put any picture into as many groups as you like and include as many pictures in each group as you like. It is your ideas that count.
>
> When you have finished a sorting, we would like you to tell us the reasons for your sorting and what it is that the pictures have *in common*. After you have sorted the pictures once, we will ask you to do it again, using any other principles you can think of. You may continue sorting as many times as you can think of categories that are useful. Please tell us whatever thoughts you may have as you are sorting the pictures.

Multiple sorting was used by Bishop (1983) to determine whether the age of buildings was significant in people's views of their surroundings. Using the set of photographs provided, thirty to thirty-five people tested did use age as a basis of sorting, but only eight used it in the first sort. Bishop was able to categorize the type of age sorting that occurred, illustrating that his subjects' understanding of building age varied greatly. From the results he was able to develop his study further. Groat (1982) used sortings of photographs of buildings to investigate how architects' ways of thinking about famous buildings differed from accountants'. Oakley (1980) asked residents of Salvation Army hostels to use labels (such as hotel, parents' home, and hospital) to sort places to stay. And Grainger (1980) had architects and clients sort for activities that a proposed building might house to establish their understandings of the building's functions.

Experience has established some basic principles for the use of multiple sorting, but other aspects need exploration. Tests so far have shown that more concrete, specific, and familiar sets of test elements yield richer results than those that are abstract and unfamiliar to subjects. In some studies, the relative distribution of elements in sorting has been linked to the extremity of views held by the sorters; assigning most elements to one or two outlying categories, for instance, was thought to indicate more strongly held views on the part of the sorter than a more equal distribution across a greater number of categories.

The significance of the order in which different sorts are made, as well as the use of only a portion of a prepared set, have yet to be investigated. Determining the number of elements and their source—usually the tester or the subject—will depend on the nature of the research: whether it is meant to explore experiences, describe or classify phenomena, or test hypotheses. Modifying the sorting technique itself holds much potential for answering research questions. Sorts can be ranked or rated to produce higher orders according to specific criteria, such as importance. People can be asked to sort for specified, as well as self-selected, criteria. Sorting one set of elements into another can be used to investigate relationships between conceptual domains. And results from group sorting, alone or in combination with or in comparison to individual sorting, may be more pertinent to some studies, provided that the tasks are simple or the groups sophisticated. Working to develop element sets themselves can produce more expertise in the understanding and promotion of useful and valid test results.

LANDSCAPE EVALUATION PARADIGMS

With increasing concern in the last several decades about conserving, regulating, and creating landscapes, environmental managers and policy makers have searched for valid means of assessing the quality of comprehensive, visually natural environments. As the number and interests of various researchers in the field—including lawyers, psychologists, land managers, and ecologists—increased, concern with appropriate theory and methodology of inquiry, and agreement among interests, decreased.

In attempting to classify various research approaches and examine their validity and utility according to theory, testing, representational capability, and legal application, Taylor, Zube, and Sell (1987) applied a mutual influence model of the human-landscape interaction process. Four paradigms were identified based on the model: *expert, psychophysical, cognitive,* and *experiential.*

Using the *expert paradigm,* landscape quality is assessed by highly skilled experts such as landscape architects and ecologists. Proponents, such as the United States Forest Service and United States Geological Survey, contend that, through their training and experience, experts have become more sensitive to the aesthetic qualities of landscapes, and therefore are better qualified than ordinary people to appreciate them. It is assumed that professional judgments will also be more objective and reliable. Testing by the Forest Service is often done according to formal design or landscape criteria, such as boundaries and edges, land form, plant cover, water elements, and focal attractions;

compositional types, feature landscape, enclosure, and focus (Litton, 1968); contrast, sequence, axis, convergence, codominance, and enframement.

Most environmental management work in North America and Great Britain has been done by experts in landscape assessment. Through and in their research, the United States Forest Service (1973) developed a set of visual manuals based on landscape architectural design principles. Visual harmony is evaluated using the three fundamental concepts of identifiable character (characteristic landscape), visual variety, and deviations from the characteristic landscape. The basic concepts are examined through three sets of criteria: *dominance elements* (Figure 1-2), *dominance principles,* such as contrast, sequence, enframement, and axis, and *variable factors,* which include motion, light, atmospheric conditions, season, distance, scale, time, and observer position. The Bureau of Land Management Visual Resources Management Program operates on a similar system, but with an added numerical rating. Both agencies use landscape factors to derive a set of Landscape Management Classes.

According to the *psychophysical paradigm,* landscape is valued for its ability to stimulate responses in observers. Based upon traditional ex-

Form

Line

Color

Texture

Figure 1-2: Dominance elements: form, color, line, and texture.

perimental psychology, psychophysical research measures the conditioned aesthetic response of observers to external and invariant properties of a landscape, which designers and managers can then manipulate in creating and enhancing environments. The approach has been used to broaden the base of landscape assessment to measure the aesthetic values of the general public: to determine what the general public finds appealing, the general public or a special interest group is tested. Much of the work in outdoor recreation landscape perception has been done according to psychophysical methods. Correlations have been drawn, for instance, between campground attractiveness and use (Huberlein & Dunwiddie, 1979). Cherem determined *senso-environmental change,* that is, movement from a forested area to a clearing, or visa versa, to be significant to hikers who used cameras to photograph areas of special scenic character in their treks (1973).

Daniel and Boster used a Scenic Beauty Estimation [SEB] method to ask respondents to rate thirty-five landscape scenes on a 1-to-10 or 1-to-9 scale (1976). Pitt and Zube used the Q-sort method of having subjects place predetermined numbers of cards into separate piles according to degrees of scenic quality, to establish the importance of topographic relief, water, agricultural elements, natural elements, the context of cultural features, and land-use covers (1979).

The key concept of the *cognitive paradigm* is that landscape has value for people because of the intellectual or social associations that they make with various settings. Rather than reacting passively to environmental stimuli, people select those aspects for which they have built up constructs, usually on the basis of visual experience. Researchers focus more on why landscapes are valued, rather than what is valued. Various assumptions about the basis for selection have been tested, among them that preference is based on an optimal number, neither too many nor too few, of features (Wohlwill & Kohn, 1976); that the human experience of landscape is related to an evolutionary reconciliation of safe refuge within the environment with retention of prospects of it (Appleton, 1975); that preference is shown for those aspects of environment that relate to the needs of the perceiver (S. Kaplan, 1979). Other researchers have investigated relationships between different cultures and landscape perception, and personality traits and landscape preference.

Most research following the cognitive paradigm has been conducted using verbal response techniques—survey questions, adjective checklists, and semantic differentials. In some experiments, standard psychological tests such as electrocardiographs and electroencephalographs have been used to measure physiological and emotional responses (stress, levels of arousal, feelings of affect, or emotional state) to various conditions in the environment.

Work within the *experiential paradigm* studies landscape values derived from active human participation in the environment. The landscape acquires meaning through the situations in which it is experienced; as those situations change, the experiences and meanings change. The paradigm is characteristic of the work of geographers, in their study of the evolution of landscapes and human activities, and phenomenologists, who consider attachments developed through recurrent use of places. Some researchers have examined the inspirational potential of landscape, its ability to produce "sublime" or "transcendent" experience, through verbal reports of their subjects or through resulting creative expressions in art and literature. Others have focused on methods of enhancing the experience of landscapes by increasing sensitivity and bases of appreciation through experience and knowledge.

Techniques used in measuring experiential values are less structured than those used in other paradigms. Because experience depends on the nature and intensity of the interaction of people and environment, most studies accept their subjects' subjective responses according to the personal criteria by which they were generated. Sources of investigation include literature, art, art history, journals, diaries, travelers' descriptions, letters, and poetry; content is examined for evidence of human values in documented perceptions.

Taylor, Zube, and Sell (1987) suggest the benefits of combining paradigms in studying, managing, and designing the landscape. The expert view is suited to describing and documenting physical components. Psychophysical studies can be used to identify those components which are most likely to be associated with scenic beauty, while the cognitive approach can provide understanding of the meaning and associations which observers attach to them. The experiential paradigm can be used to study and describe the interaction of landscapes and people, bringing together the landscape focus of the expert and psychophysical views and the human focus of the cognitive.

Before any of the paradigms is adopted for use in landscape research, each must be considered according to its theoretical basis, and also against Daniel and Vining's criteria of validity, reliability, sensitivity, and utility (1983) for evaluating measurement techniques. *Validity* is established through the actual relationship between what is purported to be measured and what is measured. *Reliability* is the consistency of results with repeated testing. *Sensitivity* is the ability of the technique to measure actual differences. *Utility* is the applicability of test results for a given group or situation. Special attention is given to the criterion of validity, since some ways of representing landscapes—line drawings, for instance—may not produce the same responses as real landscapes; likewise, some landscape simulations or surrogates may not be unbiased samples of the actual environment.

VISUAL REPRESENTATION

While it is apparent that visual images are not duplications of the environment but merely representations, there are numerous explanations concerning how images can represent the environment (Palmer, 1986). Arnheim (1954) describes a theory traditionally held by artists that the image is a faithful reproduction of the object itself; that the trained observer sees images as what they represent. Earlier theories of representation have their basis in Renaissance rational geometry, where it was believed that a perfect painting was characterized by the similarity of the depiction of light in the painting to natural illumination in the setting itself (Gibson, 1971). Recent theories suggest (Gibson, 1971) that, while the same visual information may be contained in the real environment and in a picture, they do not provide the same stimulation. Pictures record information, not sensory data (Gibson, 1979, p. 280).

Visual simulations that depict existing or potential environmental conditions are based on a number of graphic principles. These principles enable observers to perceive three-dimensional relationships from two-dimensional representations. This sensory shift from a drawing or photograph to an awareness of a real environment is based on perspective principles described by Gibson (1979) as surface layout. He suggests that we refer to surfaces as we experience them in terms of color and texture. The visual simulations are actually perspective clues that are present for stationary objects viewed with only one eye, also referred to as monocular perspective. The clues pertain to texture, size, linearity, aerial, upward location, texture shift, continuity, and transition.

> *Texture.* When a surface gradually becomes denser, it appears to recede from the observer.
> *Size.* As objects decrease in size, they appear to recede from the observer (Figure 1-3).
> *Linearity.* When objects equal in distance from each other appear to converge to a point, they recede from the observer.
> *Aerial.* Objects lose detail when their distance from the observer increases.

Figure 1-3: Contrasts of light and shade convey *trasitional* cues (Photo: Henry Sanoff).

Upward location. The horizon line appears to rise as the observer's distance increases.

Texture shift. Changes in texture density give the appearance of an occluding edge.

Continuity. When objects overlap, the simpler form is perceived as being nearer to the observer.

Transition. Sharp contrasts in light and shade reveal an edge (Figure 1-4).

Figure 1-4: Diminution in *size* as a perceptual cue (Photo: Henry Sanoff).

Motion provides an additional perspective clue. This visual information can be depicted by a sequence of pictures, or pictures seen from slightly different points. Binocular perspective, for example, is used in photogrammetry to interpret depth using stereo pairs of aerial photographs. Stereoscopes were once popular for viewing landscape scenes. Film or video simulation permits scenes to be represented in ways that still pictures cannot (Hochberg & Brooks, 1978). They provide depth cues not available in still pictures. Scenes can be represented by successive views and represent an interest level that cannot be sustained in still pictures. Environmental events can also be represented, juxtaposed, manipulated, and viewed differently than in still photographs. Action, periods of time, and the extent of space are all features that motion pictures portray, that still pictures cannot.

VISUAL CUES

Perceiving and interpreting the physical environment is a complex process involving the interaction of human physiology, development, experience, and cultural sets and values with outside stimuli. In making sense of the visual world we rely on a number of physical characteristics which define objects and their relationships in three-dimensional space. Ittleson (1960) identified the three basic components of the perceptual process, of defining "thereness and thatness," as impingement by the physical object, excitation of the physiological sensors, and assumption in the psychological realm. In simple discrimination of elements in the visual field, we rely on the interaction of characteristics or cues such as size, shape, color, brightness, position in the field, overlay, linear and aerial perspective, movement parallex, light and shade, accommodation, convergence, and stereoscopic vision. At the more complex psychosocial level, we interpret selected characteristics of the perceived environment in terms of associations and values which communicate identity and status, establishing a context and defining a situation (Rapoport, 1982).

We are well accustomed to seeing and interpreting clothing and other personal effects as indicators of identity and status. Uniformed military personnel and civil servants can be readily recognized and categorized according to unit and rank. With some instruction, the affiliation and position of different clergymen are discernable. Similarly, we learn to interpret and evaluate other "uniforms"—such as doctors' lab coats, sanitation workers' overalls, and construction workers' hard hats—which were adopted for more strictly utilitarian reasons. Through study, associations can be made between more subtle exterior physical signs or personal cues and social or cultural memberships. For instance, there are reports on the found association between hair length and the methodological disposition of psychologists (in which short hair was indicative of "tough-mindedness") and between shoe style and cultural set (with "flashier" styles characteristic of more culturally-bound wearers) (Webb et al., 1972).

Although less studied and understood, visual cues are no less common in the larger environment. Rapoport (1982) reported on a study by Duffy in 1969 of British Civil Service offices laden with physical cues specifying the relative status of occupants. Office size, carpentry, number of windows, furnishings, and other appointments were carefully correlated to each grade of civil service. Although somewhat less self-consciously, executives and academics routinely communicate their differing levels of dominance and position through furniture arrangement and office decoration (Rapoport, 1982). Other settings are less deliberately coded, but usually without consciousness people communicate status and suggest appropriate responsive behavior through inclusion and exclusion of symbolic ingredients. Through study and analysis, designers and researchers can learn how people decode their existing environments to be better able to encode new ones with desirable and meaningful associations.

The built environment is continuously transmitting messages to people. These messages convey cues for behavior which people are able to read and understand. The environment, then, has a certain meaning which is communicated and acted upon by people in diverse settings. People read environmental cues, make judgments about the occupants of settings, and act accordingly. It follows that the environment contains social, cultural, and symbolic information, and transmits many nonverbal messages that elicit appropriate behavior (Wagner, 1972). These messages play an important role in people's comprehension of the environment. People can identify the nature of places, judge their quality and status, identify settings, and know how to behave. Specific environments can be evaluated in terms of status, whether public or private, front or back, and if the cues are properly interpreted, people can act appropriately with regard to the environment or the people in it (Rapoport, 1977).

Since people act and behave differently in different settings, usually according to the behavioral norms defined by the culture, the built environment can be seen as a form of nonverbal communication. Hall (1966) distinguishes between various characteristics of a space by his descriptions of fixed feature space (walls, doors, and so on), semi-fixed feature space (furniture, furnishings, and so on), and non-fixed feature elements such as people, their facial expressions, gestures, and their proxemic relationships. The physical environment in itself, particularly through meanings attached to it, may affect people's perception of environmental quality (Sherif & Sherif, 1963).

CATEGORIZING VISUAL CUES

The residential environment that is part of everyday life has embedded within it cues about the social system which contain symbolic references that are more significant than shelter. While the way in which this type of social learning takes place has been rarely studied in detail, Sanoff's (1973) study argues that it is important to understand the classification scheme that people use to comprehend the environment as well as the meaning they are likely to draw from the categories.

Little is known about the kinds of differences that young people are apt to notice, yet it is clear that the "house" transmits cues which they use to build social categories about the nature and desirability of their environments. It also appears that everyday environmental experiences of urban and rural young people may have a very different quality, exerting a pervasive influence upon their perceptions as well as aspirations.

Kelly (1955) views perceptions of sameness and differences as the basic elements of cognitive structure. He suggests that if we discover the numbers and kinds of dimensions that are used to compare and contrast stimuli, then we shall have a framework from which to derive preferences. This exploratory study, then, began with the following questions as a basis for investigation: What kinds of perceptual cues are young people most likely to notice? Do youths from different environments differ in the criteria they use for comparison? Do they use the same criteria to compare and evaluate visual stimuli (Steinitz, 1971)?

The ability of youths to group different things discriminately and treat them as alike permits them the ability to cope with diversity of the environment. This equivalence making is part of cognitive development. Particularly through visual representation, descriptions can be made of different features of the environment. Equivalence through visual representation might more likely be accomplished by grouping items according to perceptual likeness; however, the basis for judging similarities may be more extensive.

Olver and Hornsby (1966) suggest five main modes for distinguishing equivalence: perceptible, functional, affective, nominal, and fiat. They are defined as follows:

Perceptible. The individual describes the items equivalent on the basis of immediate phenomena qualified, such as size, shape, or on the basis of location.

Functional. The individual may base equivalence on the use of function of items.

Affective. Items may be described as equivalent on the basis of an emotion they arouse or of an evaluation of them.

Nominal. Items may be grouped by a name that exists for them in the language.

Fiat. Items may be described as the same or alike without providing any further information.

While these modes are primarily based on verbal descriptions, it has been demonstrated that when using visual representations of identical functional equivalence (a house), judgments of similarity are more extensive than "perceptible," that is, they can be based on other than identifiable physical characteristics.

Brunswik (1956) has suggested that the generality of statistical results, or representativeness, may be more important than proper sampling of subjects. Representativeness of multiple-cue residential settings in this study of images of "house" was achieved by the categorization of 1500 photographs of rural North Carolina houses. Six representative categories of house types were identified, illustrated by pictures A, C, D, F, H, and J. Another six photographs were selected for their unique design characteristics compared to the more representative houses in the study locale (Figure 1-5).

The sample of 153 respondents, consisting of eleventh- and twelfth-grade students, was drawn from urban and rural settings. Location of present residence was chosen to be the dependent variable, while house description was the independent variable. In an interview setting, eighty-seven urban and sixty-six rural teenagers were asked to sort the twelve house photographs for similarities and make a preference ranking of all house types. The similarity responses were classified into seven major categories: *form, detail, quality, context, style, size,* and *status* (Table 1-1). This classification scheme was used in the content analysis of the youths' similarity structure as suggested by the cues in the house photographs.

Table 1-1. Classification of descriptive attributes (similarity criteria)

form	detail	quality	context	style	size	status
flat	brick	comfortable	isolated	plain	one-story	subdivision
gable	wood	spacious	bleak	barn	two-story	vacation
gambril	painted			rustic	small	
round	dark trim			country	large	
angular	vertical			commercial		
symmetrical	horizontal			unique		
high pitch	dormers			strange		
low pitch	columns			unusual		
rectilinear	porch			split-level		
horizontal	chimney			simple		
	windows			complex		
	shutters					

Figure 1-5: House images in rural North Carolina (Photo: Kent Carpenter/Henry Sanoff).

The free sort test was intended to elicit the most salient categories of similarities. The results of the sort indicated that the highest degree of similarity was found between house types K and L, J and F, and B and D.

The major factors accounting for the similarity between house types K and L were described as *shape, roof line,* and *surface materials,* while for house F and J, the same descriptions were used with the addition of *plain* and *ordinary.* Pictures B and D were described as *alike* primarily because of *roof line* and *shape.* A relatively larger number of urban than rural youths grouped houses A and C. House types A, E, and K were similar to the urban group because of *roof line, shape, materials, country look,* and *low income image.* The rural group described houses A and C as similar because they were both *old-fashioned, two-stories* had *long front porches, columns in front,* and similar *front windows.* Both groups suggested a strong association between G and I because of the *large windows* and use of *wood.* The rural group linked houses G and K because of the use of *wood,* while the urban group linked houses G and K because of the use of *wood* and because they looked *modern.*

From the sorting for similarities it was evident that physical criteria (*form, details,* and *size)* were the predominant criteria used as a basis for grouping houses. A majority of the teenagers, however, did select nonphysical criteria, such as *style,* at least once to group houses. The first major sort for a similarity criterion appeared to be at a "perceptible" level where comparisons were made between physical characteristics of the house *types.* The second criterion used for similarity was "affective," where groupings were made along quality dimensions. The third criterion in the free sort was "nominal," where similarities were distinguished by their name only.

In another task, the house triads, the students were presented with three house photographs and asked to select the two which were alike and explain their choice. The twelve house types were grouped into four sets of triads. The triads were intended to test the relative strength of the various categories. Therefore, the triad choices were classified into the same categories as the free sort responses. The predominant criteria for the triad association for both groups were *form* and *detail.* This further substantiates the results from the free sort task.

The students were also asked for their house type preferences and explanations of their choices. Comparing the results from both groups, house type H was preferred by a majority of the rural group, while the urban group preferred houses C and H. Both groups agreed upon *bigness* and *split level* as the reasons for their preferences. The positive attributes cited by the urban group were descriptions such as *modern, style, setting,* and *comfortable looking.* The rural group described the positive characteristics of their preferences as *big, comfortable, split level*, and *beautiful*.

There appeared to be greater agreement between groups about what is disliked than what is preferred. When comparing the reasons for similarity groupings of the houses and the reasons for the preferences, the major difference appears to be in the frequency of use of "affective" descriptions such as *style* and *status* compared to former groupings on the basis of "perceptibility."

RECOGNITION OF BUILDING TYPES

Questions related to the meaning of the environment and how people classify the environment are central to the study of visual perception. Visual images in the perceiver's mind activate selective responses in the visual perception of objects. One measure of success of building design is the ability of the designer to suggest the use or cultural significance of a building in the context of others.

The object of the following study was to establish the minimal critical properties necessary for a subject to be able to classify a building as belonging to a particular functional type. Secondary issues were whether the ability to classify a building type varies according to the amount of detail available in the design, and how the visual properties of the buildings correspond to verbal labels such as "factory," "office building," "church," "school," and so forth.

In addressing these questions, an investigation was conducted by Krampen (1979) comparing recognition performances of French-speaking subjects. Architectural students were chosen as subjects because it was believed that there is no crucial difference in the process of conceptualizing buildings as carried out by architects or consumers. (The choice of subjects would be more critical for recognizing stylistic differences between buildings of the same functional category.) The experiment consisted of a sorting process using four sets of thirty-five pictures. Three sets of pictures were traced from the original set of photographs, each containing a different degree of detail. The first set consisted only of building outlines (Figure 1-6) and certain cues acting as scale references. The second set gave indications of the number of stories (Figure 1-7), the third added windows (Figure 1-8), and the fourth set consisted of original photographs (Figure 1-9).

Subjects were asked to sort the pictures into the categories of factory, office building, tenement house, church, school, and individual home. This procedure was repeated four times until each subject was exposed to four levels of detail, from abstract drawings to a photograph. One week was allowed to elapse between each exposure to

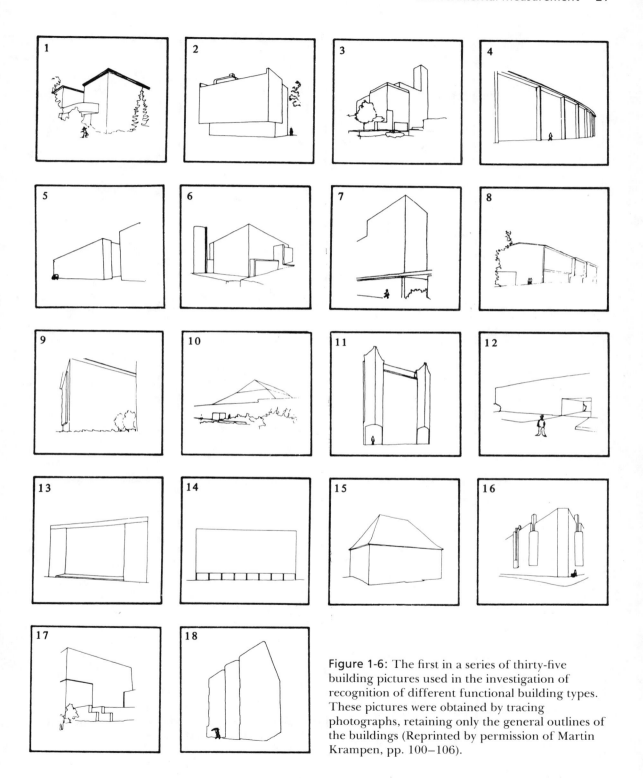

Figure 1-6: The first in a series of thirty-five building pictures used in the investigation of recognition of different functional building types. These pictures were obtained by tracing photographs, retaining only the general outlines of the buildings (Reprinted by permission of Martin Krampen, pp. 100–106).

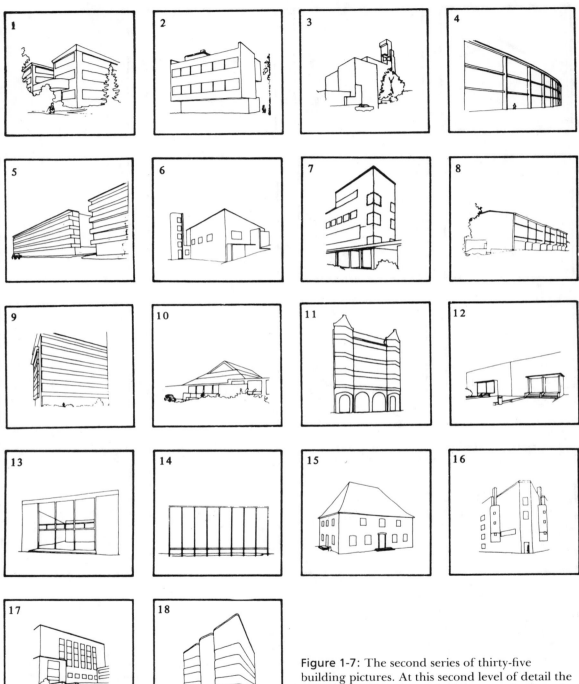

Figure 1-7: The second series of thirty-five building pictures. At this second level of detail the number of storeys in the buildings was indicated (Reprinted by permission of Martin Krampen, pp. 100–106).

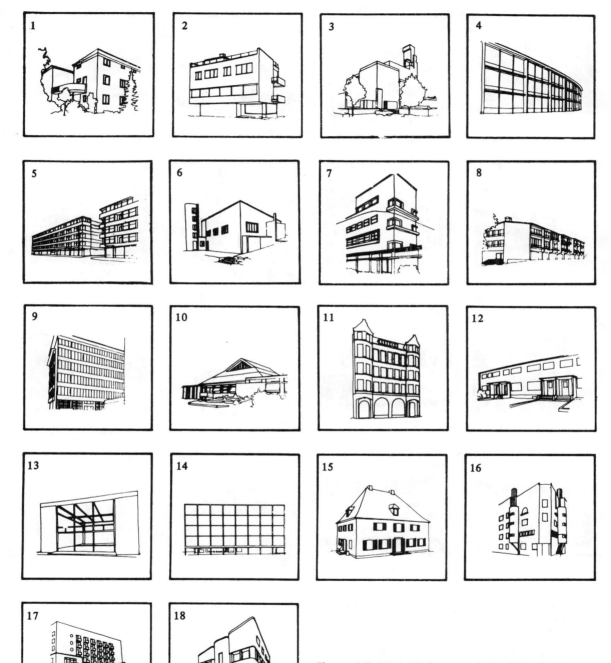

Figure 1-8: The third series of the thirty-five building pictures, offering a third level of detail: shape, number, and subdivision of windows and their distribution on the facade (Reprinted by permission of Martin Krampen, pp. 100–106).

Figure 1-9: The fourth series of thirty-five building pictures, photographs presenting the maximum level of detail (Reprinted by permission of Martin Krampen, pp. 100–106).

ensure that the subjects would not remember details of the previous exposure. In each stage the subjects were free to attribute to each category as many pictures as he or she thought belonged to it. Then the subjects were asked to rank the pictures in each category from the most to the least typical. They were then asked to select the most representative picture for each category and indicate the design features which led to this choice. Finally, they were asked to record which features were used to identify the most typical building of each category.

The results of this study indicated that the first level of detail (Figure 1-6) provided only sufficient information for the subjects to identify houses, by their small size, and one church by its dome. Additional information at the second level (Figure 1-7) about the number of stories made no appreciable difference. At the third level (Figure 1-8), the design feature which enabled the subjects to supply five of the six categories of building types was the number, size, and distribution of windows. Only at the fourth level (Figure 1-9), the photographs, was complete classification possible. The presence of detail exhibited in the photographs seemed essential for successful classification of a building, particularly for basic volumes in the form of a simple rectangular box, without addition of secondary volumes (for example, a steeple) or other protrusions such as balconies.

An examination of the pictures within the various categories suggests that size, complexity of building silhouette, and the number, size, form, and distribution of windows were the features used by subjects to classify the photographs. The three principal variables for describing the buildings were size, shape, and windows.

The study indicates that the most significant exterior cues for conveying information about a building's function are size (defined by the number, size, and distribution of windows in each story and the horizontal or vertical extensions of the building), homogeneity of building volume and form, and various stylistic features.

ATTRIBUTES OF RESIDENTIAL ENVIRONMENTS

People perceive the visual world and respond to it through sensory mechanisms that have been triggered by some form of environmental stimulation. There is evidence indicating that individuals have a requirement for sensory intake of appreciably varied perceptions and that an extreme lack of external stimulation can have deleterious consequences. As A. E. Parr (1966) succinctly states, "the variety inherent in the natural environment has been succeeded by a far smaller selection of much more vigorously repetitive forms which has recently been reduced to even greater uniformity by explicit architectural doctrine. A loss of diversity, particularly in the visually perceived environment, is one universal, and still continuing trend in the transition from virgin country to city streets."

Rene Dubos (1967), indicating that "we must shun uniformity of the environment," states that the present "creeping monotony" can be overcome by "creating as many diverse environments as possible." While diversity in the designed environment can give rise to sensory stimulation, a more homogeneously uniform environment may discourage any sensory arousal. Therefore, judgments of satisfaction with the physical environment are manifestations of aroused visual stimuli sustaining the interest of the perceiver.

Knowledge of people's visual comprehension of their physical environment is primarily the responsibility of *environmental psychology*, a science which may be defined as the psychological study of behavior as it relates to the everyday physical environment (Craik, 1968). How people perceive their everyday physical world, the distinctions they make about it, and the significant factors affecting comprehension, are all questions of great importance to architects and urban designers and deserve immediate attention. It seems evident that knowledge of the perceptual responses elicited by visual stimuli can be gained through the use of psychological theory and testing techniques.

Environmental psychologists have conducted many laboratory studies using controlled visual stimuli and corresponding responses. Berlyne's (1960) experiments in *complexity* and *novelty* led him to conclude that the more complex the stimuli, the stronger the investigatory reflex elicited. He also states that diversity, complexity, novelty, and ambiguity in a composition are conditions which lead to *arousal* and *attention*. Order, organization, symmetry, and repetition keep arousal within moderate and tolerable bounds. An aesthetic product has to accomplish two things: (1) gain (and maintain) the attention of an audience, and (2) keep arousal within limits. Hebb (1949) describes the *stimulus field* as "requiring some familiarity, yet some novelty to sustain the interest of the perceiver." Pfaffman (1960) states that sensory stimulation plays a significant role in motivating as well as guiding behavior, "in controlling behavior for the pleasure of sensation," as he says.

According to much of the literature of experimental psychology (Miller, Galanter, & Pribram, 1960), the primary conditions for human sensory stimulation associated with visual environments are that the environments be continual, varied, and patterned. There also exists a body of experimental literature to assert that nonfulfillment of any of these conditions produces stress and will ultimately become intolerable. Studies dealing with various forms of sensory deprivation (Day,

1965) demonstrate conclusively the need for both continuity and novelty. They indicate that exploratory behavior regarding novelty seeking, fantasy, and preference for moderately nonredundant figures over highly redundant ones begins when there is not enough visual information available. The awareness of the need for greater perceptual interest in the physical world has been expressed by Stea (1965), Vigier (1965), and Rapoport and Kantor (1967). Thus, the approach presented is predicated on the notion that physical forms are no longer ends in themselves, but means employed to bring the designed environment into equilibrium with human systems.

The problem, then, is to determine people's affective responses to architecture or environment—that is, how people perceive their environment. Studies of environmental perception involve four groups of variables (Craik, 1968): observers, modes of observation, environments, and attributes of environments. The experiment described here focuses on the visual attributes of the environment, isolating all other stimulus inputs, such as auditory or olfactory, in order to ascertain the degree to which judgments based only on visual attributes will influence satisfaction. The intent of this research is to open avenues of exploration for the systematic analysis of responses relating to the visual environment. The specific aims of the experiments are (1) to assess the relation between visual satisfaction and complexity, ambiguity, and novelty, and (2) to develop a model which can be utilized by designers to describe the desired attributes (Sanoff, 1974b).

The Experiment

Generally, there are two ways in which we can examine the structure of the physical world, or two fundamental operations for sorting out meaningful relations among words: *contrast* and *grouping*. Attributes can be isolated so that the physical world can be ordered with respect to attribute. Or, alternatively, descriptions can be made in terms of collections of similarities of attributes. This experiment focuses on the ordering of attributes, though it is well recognized that other associative techniques could be developed in future experiments.

Assessment techniques can be used to permit expressions of varied subtle reactions to environmental phenomena through verbal descriptions of the images they evoke. Descriptive judgments are elicited using a bipolar scale of opposite attributes referred to as a semantic differential (Osgood, Suci, & Tannenbaum, 1957).

In order to identify the appropriate attributes for study, an ad hoc list was drawn from the terms most frequently used by designers in their judgments and descriptions of the environment. The polar

opposite terms selected for analysis incorporated a consensus of opinions
about visual attributes; however, the word list is by no means exhaus-
tive or comprehensive. Since the terms were identified by professional
designers, the list undoubtedly reflected a professional bias. The
words involve a considerable range of meaning varying with time,
place, and context of perception and with the background and experience of the respondent.

Several of the terms used to denote properties were value-laden. To
many, *symmetry* has a negative, and *assymetry* a positive, connotation.
Novel may be viewed more favorably than *common; static* and *dynamic*
seem to be bad and good, respectively. In spite of the emotional significance of the words selected, the technique can elicit a large number
of specific judgments about a complex aesthetic stimulus.

Descriptions of the attributes of residential environments were
elicited from thirty experts (architects) in research and design. The
architects represented a national sample drawn from the Directory of
Behavior and Environmental Design (Studer & Stea, 1967). Environmental displays consisting of four strip photographs of different residential settings were presented to the subjects, representing typical
anonymous developer projects that were popular during their period.
Two photographs represented San Francisco's "carpenter Victorian"
period of the 1880's, (Figure 1-10) and two photographs characterized
1960's residential development in North Carolina. All residential
scenes depicted attached rental apartment units. The study was also
intended to test the sensitivity of the instrument, that is, to see if the
semantic differential scale could distinguish between subtle differences
as well as obvious stylistic differences.

An analysis of the adjective pairs that described differences between
photographs revealed cluster patterns associated with settings that
were liked and disliked. The clusters or factors were described as "affective," "judgmental," and "descriptive." For example, affective responses to the photographs elicited comments such as *interest,
exhilarated, like, satisfaction, novel, dynamic,* and *stimulating.* Judgmental
responses were reflected in terms such as *clarity, peaceful, ordered, relaxed,* and *softness.* Finally, the descriptive pattern was associated with
words such as *uniform, unity, formal,* and *symmetry.* The attributes of
preferred environments appeared to be *complexity, stimulating, sensuous,
dynamic,* and *roughness.* The less-preferred environments were described by the attributes *simplicity, universal, asymmetry, unobtrusiveness,
common, static,* and *uniform* (Figure 1-11).

The responses to the turn-of-the-century residential settings were
significantly more positive than those to the 1960's settings. Of the
four photographs presented, there appeared to have been the greatest

a

b

c

d

Figure 1-10: Residential street facades A, B, C, & D: (Photos: Henry Sanoff).

29

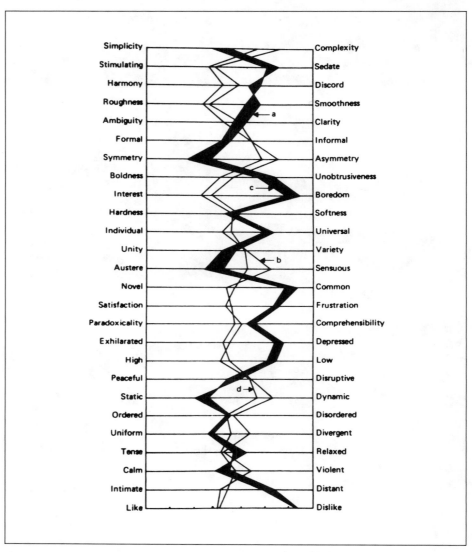

Figure 1-11: Arithmetic mean distribution for all street facades emphasizing the polarization between the San Francisco (white) and Raleigh (black) scenes.

difference of opinion about the most preferred, and the greatest agreement about the most disliked settings. This quality of ambiguity, or multiple meanings reflected by positive responses to the older settings, and associations with attributes of *complexity* and *novelty*, support Berlyne's conclusions (1966). The attributes *interest* and *satisfaction*, two important consumer variables, were positively associated with "affective" judgments of the residential settings.

It is important to recognize, however, that response information was response-defined. That is, the respondents' ratings were analyzed to provide information about the respondents and their perception, more so than identifiable characteristics of the environmental scenes (Gregson, 1964).

CHARACTERIZING HISTORIC ARCHITECTURE

In studying significant concentrations of older historic buildings, professionals such as architectural historians and architects typically identify or define features that relate buildings to or distinguish them from established historical typologies or styles. Seeking instead to understand the symbolic cultural meaning that a particular vernacular building tradition might have for local residents, an anthropologist and an architect developed a method for documenting physical characteristics that conveyed the uniqueness of a place (Low & Ryan, 1985). The study, sponsored by the National Trust for Historic Preservation, was intended to suggest culturally-appropriate design guidelines for preserving, modifying, or infilling the existing environment.

The rural township of Oley, Pennsylvania, contains the nation's densest concentration of early stone farmsteads and largest collection of handmade tile roofs. The area, which was settled in the early eighteenth century by German farmers, was feeling the impact of urbanization in nearby Reading in development of an increasing number of suburban enclaves. Concerned also about the effect of local quarrying and a growing population, a group of residents sought an assessment through the Berks County Conservancy and the National Trust's Rural Conservation Demonstration Program. The Oley Resource Conservation Project began in 1980 with a survey of historic buildings, an analysis of ecological factors, and a community survey. Teammates Setha M. Low and William P. Ryan used the various study results as a basis for their research plan to document local perceptions of "Oleyness."

In the survey of historic buildings, researchers relied on presence or absence of applied details like lintels, keystones, transoms, quoins, shutters, cornices and pediments and porches at the main entrance in categorizing buildings as *Georgian* (regardless of age) or *vernacular;* in fact, the buildings shared a common building material and similar massing. In order to determine which elements held key local identity, Low and Ryan prepared drawings of variations of typical building details, which they pre-tested and modified for easier differentiation before presentation to a representative cross section of the community

(Figures 1-12, 1-14). Drawings rather than photographs were chosen so that the number of architectural elements presented in each combination could be controlled. The elements investigated included: windows, wall openings, shutters, exterior material (Figure 1-12), main facade, gable, chimney location (Figure 1-13), porches, roof detailing, overall mass of farmhouse (Figure 1-14), and roof accessories.

Respondents to the Oley Image Study, which included farmers, businessmen, housewives, and community leaders, were asked to cite examples in each category which were

• most like farmhouses/farmsteads in the Oley Valley;
• least like farmhouses/farmsteads in the Oley Valley;
• among the remaining drawings, like farmhouses/farmsteads in the Oley Valley.

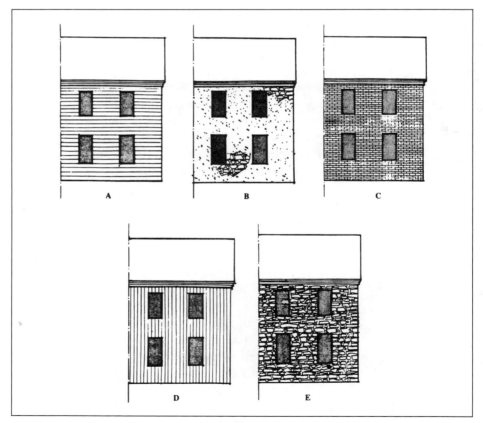

Figure 1-12: Variations in exterior materials in buildings in Oley, Pennsylvania. A. Wood siding B. Stucco C. Brick D. Wood siding E. Stone (Reprinted by permission of Setha Low).

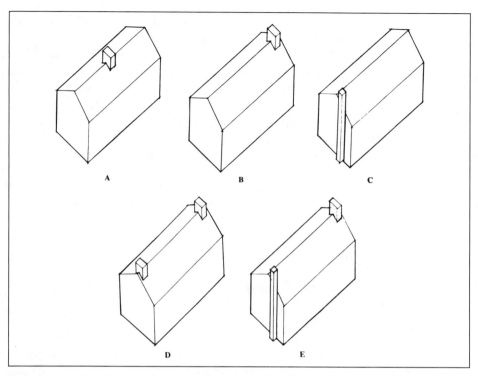

Figure 1-13: Variations in chimney location: number, location, and types of chimneys (Reprinted by permission of Setha Low).

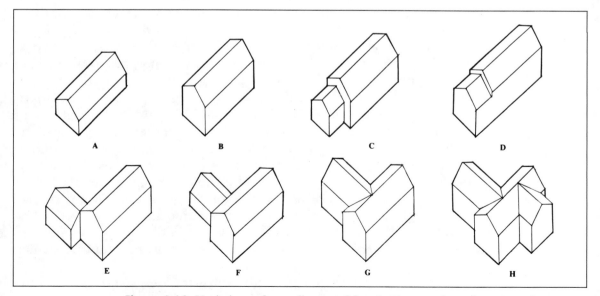

Figure 1-14: Variations of overall mass of farmhouse: number of storeys; plan configuration (Reprinted by permission of Setha Low).

It was observed that those elements which were larger and most conspicuous—wall materials, chimneys, dormers, and volumes—elicited the most rapid decisions, while smaller details—shutters, wall openings—provoked more preliminary questions about style and appropriateness rather than immediate responses. Commenting on the category "chimneys," one respondent said that this question was easiest because these elements were something that "you would notice without looking for them." The degree of "Oleyness" is most clearly represented in the architectural elements shown in Figures E, D, and G.

The study suggested that those aspects of the environment that were easily observed, and not necessarily tied to the conceptual and formal language of styles, were more powerful indicators of local identity and place.

PHOTO INTERVIEWING

While there has been an emerging awareness of the social life of communities (Cooper, 1975; Marcus Sarkissian, 1986), less attention has been given to the physical features from which people construct community life (Suttles, 1972). In studying such socioeconomic constructs, Wagner (1979) poses a crucial question: How can we investigate the manner in which people perceive their world—for indeed it is within "perceived space" that communities are formed—without structuring their own preconceptions within categories of our own? In an interview situation, for example, how can we ask questions without having those questions themselves organize the perceptions of those we interview?

In the planned residential community of Twin Rivers, New York, resident perception of this community was explored through photo interviewing. A set of seventeen photographs was selected for the study, including images of the major housing types; a burned apartment; recycling bins in the shopping center parking lot; an ambiguous warning sign; and a variety of other images that seemed to capture the essential visual and physical features of the community. The photographs were presented to forty randomly selected adults and twenty-one teenagers. For the first ten photographs, questions were based on the subjects' knowledge and location of the setting, while for the remaining photographs, questions related to meaning were asked. The researcher was concerned with the process by which individual perceptions would contribute to a more general sense of community in which Twin Rivers residents lived.

Four strategies were identified by which residents "recognized" the subject of a photograph: familiarity or knowing the thing itself; context or deduction from surrounding features in the photograph; analysis or deduction from familiar design; and guessing. It was found that different strategies were used with different photographs. Similarly, the recognitive process varied by photograph and not by the subject of the photograph. The comparison of townhouse photos A and B (Figure 1-15) suggests that when strong contextual elements are available, as the lake in photo B, they will be used.

Comparison of responses to these two photographs have important implications for resident perceptions of Twin Rivers. The community was designed to contain similar buildings which would give the community a distinctive and uniform visual character. This has been achieved, although the residents' knowledge of the community is based upon analysis of detail, since there is a general lack of dominant landmarks or distinctive site planning.

In addition to investigating processes of familiarity and recognition, the photo interviews were used to elicit evaluative comments from residents about their community. The photographs most likely to arouse negative comments were those depicting unaesthetic views of the environment, such as recycling bins or the burned-out apartment. The photographs generating positive evaluation were of the lake and school. When asked to select the best, the worst, and the most typical view of Twin Rivers, the lake and school emerged as the best, while the townhouses in photo A were seen as most typical. The burned-out apartment and recycling bins were top contenders for the worst of Twin Rivers. A closer look at the townhouses in photo A also includes automobiles and parking facilities, while photos of the other townhouses do not. For the Twin River residents, the car and townhouse are closely interconnected, and the two together form their image of what is typical to the community.

a   b

Figure 1-15: (a) Typical townhouse; (b) Townhouse with contextual element (Photos: Jon Wagner).

It is important to note that the observations were based on resident responses to photographs of various features of their environment, and not on the features themselves. Nevertheless, the photo interviews offered a technique for exploring and recording residents' perceptions of the community in which they live.

It is evident, then, that people interpret the identity and meaning of their environment from the interaction of, and their interaction with, a wide variety of physical features, only some of which are intended parts of conscious design. The extent to which we can learn how and on what basis people perceive their surroundings can influence our decisions and enable us to accomplish for others the intent as well as the form of design.

2

IMAGEABILITY

Buildings have certain qualities that give them a high probability of evoking a strong image in any given observer (Lynch, 1960). Characteristics like shape, color, or arrangement enable the making of vividly identified mental images of the environment. Imageability is a recurring message for designers and environment-behavior researchers (Hunt, 1985). Lynch (1960) wrote that mental images are the result of a two-way process. We all consciously look for nonverbal cues in buildings, streets, and landscapes, for we know that these cues have something to say about the values of the people who own and occupy them. Newman (1972) states that meaning of buildings to residents played a role in both the failure of Pruitt Igoe and the reduction of crime in other public housing.

In a way similar to that in which our clothes, hair style and length, cars, and houses differentiate us from our neighbors, buildings can symbolically represent an attitude about what is taking place inside. Often however, when we have thought about symbols and meanings in relationship to the environment, it has been in reference to monumental buildings, particularly religious and civic. Yet the more common artifacts of a society, including its buildings and settlements, give us a better understanding of the past. In fact, we are more aware of how buildings in primitive cultures expressed underlying values and beliefs than we are about the same phenomenon in our own society (Rapoport, 1969).

Building and street form convey an environmental message reflecting the inner life, activities, and social conceptions of those who influenced the form, in association with the actions and value of the users (Figure 2-1). Those associations change with time. As a society, we have a tendency to reevaluate the meaning and desirability of buildings rather rapidly. Old factories and warehouses that were considered

No personality; dormers; too "boxy"; family compound?; looks like an office building or real estate office.

Lines are wonderful; aesthetic looking; great in Miami, but not in Elizabeth City; it will be dated; too stylized; would fit a variety of arts in our area; probably more modern than the surroundings; too modern; there is a lobby, I'm sure; seemingly I like this one; very inviting to me; looks like a stadium; maybe okay for a huge city; car dealer? roller rink? dance hall?

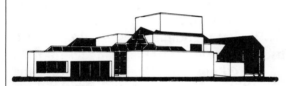

Nuclear plant looking--no warmth; too modern; functional, but too "modern"; i.e., stylized; this could be very utilitarian, but too complex; little wasted space, most utilitarian; gives need additional height in center; would give some variety; art building on campus; like this one; best of six.

Heavy, overwhelming; beach home; fits Elizabeth City; timeless charm and warmth; this design suits Elizabeth City; is more similar to immediate surroundings; chalet; Nags Head revisted.

eyesores and financial liabilities thirty years ago have become valued for their durability and their history and have been restored and renovated into useful and successful business ventures. Yet we also see the creation of new buildings whose form expresses no particular function, like banks that look like colonial homes, restaurants that look like gas stations, and apartment buildings that look like insurance buildings. Only when we understand the associations that certain forms and features have acquired through time can we interpret intended translations and mutations.

Barn look; next to a factory, great!; looks like a "smoke stack" on a factory; too modern; no good; factory; looks like a private home; house (with two-car garage; modern home.

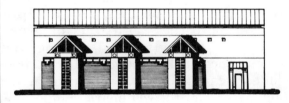

Okay; Wachovia, Texaco; too square; like a discount store front; Best, Inc.?

Figure 2-1: Building image ideas: Form studies are generated early in the programming process to sensitize clients to the interrelatedness of form and function (Drawing: H. Sanoff).

Numerous studies have examined the effect of meaning on environmental response. Groat (1982), Nasar (1989), Hershberger and Cass (1974), and Purcell (1986) report that architects differ from non-architects in the constructs they use to evaluate buildings and in their evaluation of buildings. It is evident that people may infer emotional and other qualities from style, which Rapoport (1982) describes as *pragmatic meaning*. For those with an interest in architecture that communicates desirable meanings, continued studies of meaning inferred from style is important.

CONTEXTUAL INFILL

Relating new infill buildings to existing urban settings is an issue in design practice and public policy. What specific design features influence people's perception of how well a building fits its context?

In a study of contextual compatability (Groat, 1988), color photographs of various urban scenes were shown to experts and non-experts. The twenty-five photographs presented a variety of urban scenes, each of which included both a recently designed infill building and several of the immediately adjacent buildings. Groat noted that "The primary basis for the selection of the particular buildings was that they would represent the broadest possible range of contextual-design strategies as identified through the use of a conceptual framework." An essential feature of this framework is that it distinguishes among design attributes according to the degree of control that the architect is typically able to exercise over them.

The selection of the urban scenes involved an initial review of the professional literature, procurement of color photographs, and a preliminary sorting of infill design approaches. Two pairs of expert judges evaluated the tentative set of photographs on a rating scale according to the predetermined conceptual framework. The components of the framework included site organization, or the pattern that a building imposes on the site; massing, or the volumetric composition of a building; and facade design, which is used to mean the surface treatment of the shell of the building. Each photograph received a score from the judges. The final set of photographs was chosen to reflect the broadest range of design strategies as well as photographic clarity. The choice of color photographs was based on the findings of empirical studies that have explored the validity of simulation media. Considered together, these studies have shown a high correlation between responses to color photographs and the real environment (Hershberger & Cass, 1974; Howard, Mlynarski, & Sauer, 1972; Seaton & Collins, 1972; and Feimer, 1984).

The interviews were conducted with seventy-three non-architects at three locations in the Midwest, and experts from Milwaukee, all of whom responded to the contextual compatibility of the twenty-five buildings. The experts were twenty-four individuals from design review commissions in the Milwaukee area. Each respondent was asked to rank order the twenty-five urban scenes according to his or her preference for the contextual relationship. The rank order was based on the extent to which they liked or disliked the relationship between the infill building and the surrounding context.

The composite rank orders for the expert and non-architect groups

Figure 2-2: East Cambridge Savings Bank Addition, East Cambridge, Massachusetts. Charles G. Hilgenhurst and Associates (Photo: Patricia Gill).

demonstrated that their preference judgments were very similar. The findings revealed that "the physical features that seem to contribute most significantly to the perception of compatibility have to do with facade design, as opposed to either site organization or massing; and that the most preferred contextual relationships were those that embody a high degree of replication" (Groat, 1988). Buildings that only replicate site organization and massing patterns—but not facade design features—were usually not seen as contextually compatible. Replication implied a mixture of traditional and contemporary qualities where significant design elements, such as facade design features, were replicated.

The example of the East Cambridge Savings Bank addition, by Hilgenhurst & Associates of Boston (Figure 2-2), was the most well liked by the respondents, and they commented that they appreciated the contemporary qualities of the glass link and the replicate features of the wall segment. Innovative features such as those exhibited in the

Figure 2-3: The Alumni Center, University of Michigan, Ann Arbor, Michigan. Hugh Newell Jacobsen (Photo: John Rahaim).

University of Michigan Alumni Center by Jacobson (Figure 2-3), were imaginative reinterpretations of traditional facades. The non-architects actually seemed to prefer buildings that expressed a character of their own to those that were seen merely as undistinguished imitations of the original.

The results of the study confirmed that non-architects generally find the starkness of modernist architecture incompatible with its classical predecessors (Figure 2-4). Although there is a preference for the richness of detail typical of older buildings, the respondents desired moderation in facade detail, which is manifest in their dislike of features, which are perceived as busy or confusing or inappropriate to their surroundings. The design strategies of the least preferred relationships were characterized by a relatively high degree of contrast. This was the case with the addition to the Allen Memorial Museum (Figure 2-5).

The investigation also suggests that aesthetic judgments of contextual design revealed a higher level of consistency among diverse groups than is suggested in the architectural literature.

Figure 2-4: Portland Public Services Building, Portland, Oregon. Michael Graves (Photo: Francis Downing).

Figure 2-5: Allen Memorial Art Museum Addition, Oberlin College, Oberlin, Ohio. Venturi and Rauch (Photo: Courtesy of Venturi, Rauch, and Scott Brown).

RESIDENTIAL CONTEXT

People take pride in places that have special meaning for them. This may be due to some unique quality, such as a view, a particular building, or an old tree. All streets have a history, though that may not always be evident to all observers. A street's history can be discovered, revived, or revealed, and its present history can be recorded, underscoring identity as a distinctive place rather than as a channel.

Residential streets and buildings in particular convey both wholesale cultural attitudes and individual expressions. Neighborhoods, especially as they evolve over time, are the environmental expression of similarities and differences reflected by clothing, hair style, and cars. Houses both ally us to and differentiate us from our neighbors, and symbolically represent an attitude about what is taking place inside.

"A house consists of a body of images that give mankind proof or illusions of stability" (Bachelard, 1964). Part of this stability is a sense of continuity with the past. Many intervening changes may have occurred, but a prevailing sense of history embodied in a building or place gives roots to this sense of stability and security. As the rate of change in society increases, so does the value we place on the old.

The Australian terrace house is a form of anonymous architecture of the late nineteenth century. Taken for granted at that time, it is an icon of history, inviting modern comparisons but having no modern equivalent (Irving, 1985). It is an urban vernacular, important to Australian design history. "Terrace" is used to describe all attached houses, small and large, which are unique to Australia, but not unlike the town house of North America. Terrace suggests a row, or a group of houses, single or two-storied, designed as a whole, as a piece of the street. The terraced streets contain many variations but have an overall distinctive character that comes from their collective facades.

Verandahs and balconies are strongly associated with terrace houses. One of the ways that developers of that period provided a unified appearance for their properties was to add iron decoration, or stucco verandahs or balconies. The balconies were primarily a decorative element and were widely applied because of their sales appeal (Figure 2-6). The use of iron ornamentation in Australia was fostered by nostalgic memories of the British homeland. Using familiar, traditional architectural forms over many decades, developers of the terrace house established a number of interesting variations upon the basic arrangement (Figure 2-7). In their day they suited the investors, the landlords, the occupants, and the community.

Changing land use and building use through redevelopment, however, are integral to the history of residential areas, Melbourne

Figure 2-6: Australian terrace house (Photo: Henry Sanoff).

included. Layers of change over time are often detectable as they conceal or contrast with original facades (Sanoff, 1988). In addition, poor maintenance has caused many of the old terrace houses to fall into disrepair, often making demolition inevitable. In such circumstances, there are usually no mechanisms available for deciding upon the most appropriate use of vacant property.

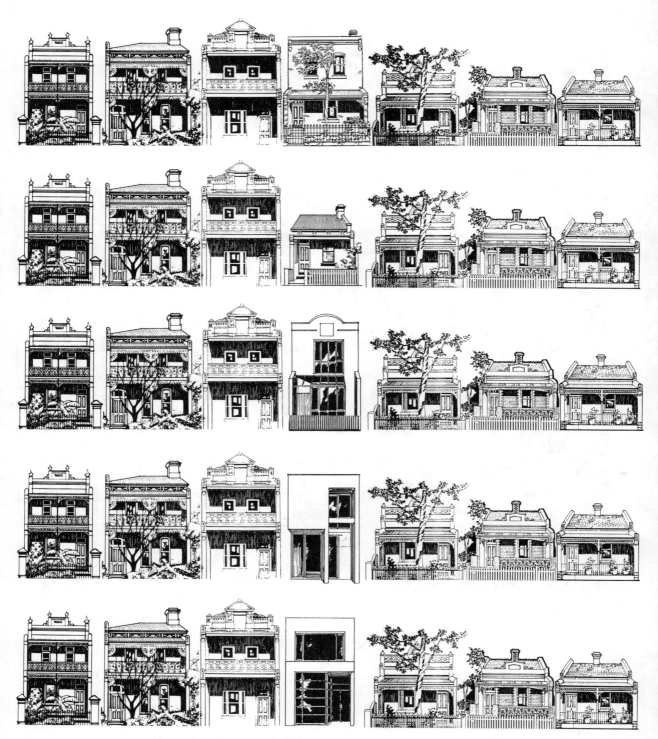

Figure 2-7: An expanded view of several terrace house infill options. The street facade contains an open slot to permit each option to be slid in place (Drawing: Henry Sanoff).

BEST FIT SLIDE RULE

The Best Fit Slide Rule (Figure 2-8) is a discussion tool designed to examine infill solutions and their consequences (Sanoff, 1978). It was developed as a strategy for discussion among public officials, land owners, professionals, and citizens' groups of the consequences of various infill options. The technique brings to light the numerous social and economic concepts that need to be understood by various interest groups in order to assure that an infill solution is appropriate for a residential setting.

The slide rule is most effectively used in small group settings where participants make individual choices, defend their decisions, and reach consensus about the most appropriate fit. Small groups enable all participants to contribute to the discussion and learn about each others' viewpoints. The process requires each group member to select one of thirteen options for the infill of a residential street. The choices include a high rise building, a commercial building, a historic adaptation, and modern buildings (Figure 2-8) reflecting different aesthetic philosophies. Participants then try to maintain their positions and debate them, but the final goal of the exercise is a solution that is acceptable to the group. Seeking the "best fit" can generate discussion about what is valued in a particular design situation. Since the participants respond to a design situation with different values and beliefs, the exercise offers the opportunity for participants to share those differences and learn from each other. Participants use the game props to clarify and reconcile differences.

Developing an awareness of the complex issues pertaining to infill, through an abstract exercise, can enable community members to focus on the social, economic, and visual implications of changing the fabric of an existing residential setting. The technique of using a hypothetical street as a stimulus for generating a discussion of important issues permits all participants to learn from each other without being encumbered with and confounded by the personal, political, economic, and site constraints of a real situation. The visual impact of the images is significant in conveying connotations usually associated with building alternatives.

Another infill activity that explores the space between groups of buildings is one that considers house placement (Bishop, 1977). Factors that are important in inserting a new house between other houses are distance between houses, distance from street (setback), and parking. Figure 2-9 offers possible solutions to house placement. Each of the examples should be considered, and reasons given why they would or would not work. The diagrams also suggest design variations which include form, shape, and setback differences. Bishop also developed

Figure 2-8: An expanded view of several building-use infill options (Drawing: Greg Centeno and Henry Sanoff).

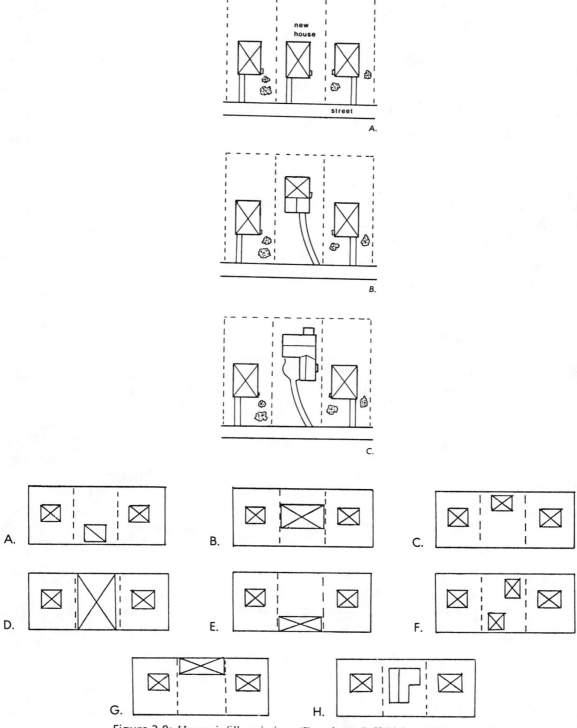

Figure 2-9: House infill variations (Drawings: Jeff Bishop, Bishop Davison O'Rourke, Bristol).

an infill exercise where the participant is the designer. It is based on his observation of people's negative reactions to many new buildings added to an existing street. In this exercise a typical British urban streetscape is shown prior to the demolition of a major building (Figure 2-10a). Figure 2-10b is a drawing given to the participant to complete. This task stresses the identification of the most significant architectural characteristics that would make a new solution suitable for the streetscape. The participant is required to consider the choice of materials, details, and the basic form of the facade, and how it corresponds to the surrounding buildings.

ENVIRONMENTAL CHARACTER

Often when we think about symbols and meaning in relation to the environment, we restrict ourselves to monumental buildings, particularly religious and civic (Rapoport, 1982). Since all building form conveys messages reflecting the inner life, actions, and social conceptions of the occupants, it is necessary to re-evaluate the meaning and desirability of existing buildings as suitable for new uses.

Various approaches can be used to heighten people's awareness of building image. In the town of Kinston, North Carolina, a public workshop was held in which residents could evaluate the desirability of four alternative vacant buildings for housing the future community arts center. Through a series of comparative drawings, it was possible to convey changes to the character of each building after it had undergone specific design modifications (Figure 2-11). Arts council members rated each alternative using a prepared list of polar opposite adjectives. The adjectives were selected from an extensive list of descriptors used most frequently in describing buildings (Kasmar, 1988). Further, since the adjective list was aimed at distinguishing differences between the images, the most effective descriptors would be "judgmental," such as *interesting, exciting,* and *imaginative* (Sanoff, 1974).

The comparative profiles shown in Figure 2-12 were based on the statistical mean calculated from the individual ratings of the twenty-six participants. Comparing the results of the profile, it can be seen that facades A and C were the most *liked,* though A was thought to be the most *beautiful, fashionable, inviting,* and *pleasant.* Facade D, the largest of the four buildings, was perceived as being the most adequate in size, *impressive, imaginative,* and also *liked,* but to a lesser degree than were Facades A and C.

This technique was effective from the participants' viewpoint because they were able to examine future building images, have an expanded vocabulary for describing the physical environment, and most

Figure 2-10a: Existing streetscape (Drawings: Jeff Bishop, Bishop Davison O'Rourke, Bristol).

Figure 2-10b: Streetscape containing a space for the infill design (Drawings: Jeff Bishop, Bishop Davison O'Rourke, Bristol).

We are going to examine the image of the building or its facade. You are provided with four building alternatives. We have collected a list of descriptive words and their opposites that can be used to classify each Arts Center facade.

Place one checkmark between each pair of adjectives that describe your feeling about the facade. For example:

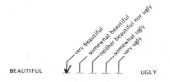

BEAULIFUL — — — — — UGLY

PROPOSED FACADE A

ADEQUATE SIZE	—	—	—	—	INADEQUATE SIZE
BEAUTIFUL	—	—	—	—	UGLY
CHEERFUL	—	—	—	—	GLOOMY
COMPLEX	—	—	—	—	SIMPLE
EXCITING	—	—	—	—	UNEXCITING
FASHIONABLE	—	—	—	—	UNFASHIONABLE
IMPRESSIVE	—	—	—	—	UNIMPRESSIVE
INVITING	—	—	—	—	REPELLING
LARGE	—	—	—	—	SMALL
PLEASANT	—	—	—	—	UNPLEASANT
FRIENDLY	—	—	—	—	UNFRIENDLY
IMAGINATIVE	—	—	—	—	UNIMAGINATIVE
INTERESTING	—	—	—	—	BORING
VARIETY	—	—	—	—	MONOTONY
LIKE	—	—	—	—	DISLIKE

PROPOSED FACADE B

ADEQUATE SIZE	—	—	—	—	INADEQUATE SIZE
BEAUTIFUL	—	—	—	—	UGLY
CHEERFUL	—	—	—	—	GLOOMY
COMPLEX	—	—	—	—	SIMPLE
EXCITING	—	—	—	—	UNEXCITING
FASHIONABLE	—	—	—	—	UNFASHIONABLE
IMPRESSIVE	—	—	—	—	UNIMPRESSIVE
INVITING	—	—	—	—	REPELLING
LARGE	—	—	—	—	SMALL
PLEASANT	—	—	—	—	UNPLEASANT
FRIENDLY	—	—	—	—	UNFRIENDLY
IMAGINATIVE	—	—	—	—	UNIMAGINATIVE
INTERESTING	—	—	—	—	BORING
VARIETY	—	—	—	—	MONOTONY
LIKE	—	—	—	—	DISLIKE

PROPOSED FACADE C

ADEQUATE SIZE	—	—	—	—	INADEQUATE SIZE
BEAUTIFUL	—	—	—	—	UGLY
CHEERFUL	—	—	—	—	GLOOMY
COMPLEX	—	—	—	—	SIMPLE
EXCITING	—	—	—	—	UNEXCITING
FASHIONABLE	—	—	—	—	UNFASHIONABLE
IMPRESSIVE	—	—	—	—	UNIMPRESSIVE
INVITING	—	—	—	—	REPELLING
LARGE	—	—	—	—	SMALL
PLEASANT	—	—	—	—	UNPLEASANT
FRIENDLY	—	—	—	—	UNFRIENDLY
IMAGINATIVE	—	—	—	—	UNIMAGINATIVE
INTERESTING	—	—	—	—	BORING
VARIETY	—	—	—	—	MONOTONY
LIKE	—	—	—	—	DISLIKE

PROPOSED FACADE D

ADEQUATE SIZE	—	—	—	—	INADEQUATE SIZE
BEAUTIFUL	—	—	—	—	UGLY
CHEERFUL	—	—	—	—	GLOOMY
COMPLEX	—	—	—	—	SIMPLE
EXCITING	—	—	—	—	UNEXCITING
FASHIONABLE	—	—	—	—	UNFASHIONABLE
IMPRESSIVE	—	—	—	—	UNIMPRESSIVE
INVITING	—	—	—	—	REPELLING
LARGE	—	—	—	—	SMALL
PLEASANT	—	—	—	—	UNPLEASANT
FRIENDLY	—	—	—	—	UNFRIENDLY
IMAGINATIVE	—	—	—	—	UNIMAGINATIVE
INTERESTING	—	—	—	—	BORING
VARIETY	—	—	—	—	MONOTONY
LIKE	—	—	—	—	DISLIKE

Figure 2-11: Building character studies (Marillia DoVal, Li Shan Lee, & Henry Sanoff).

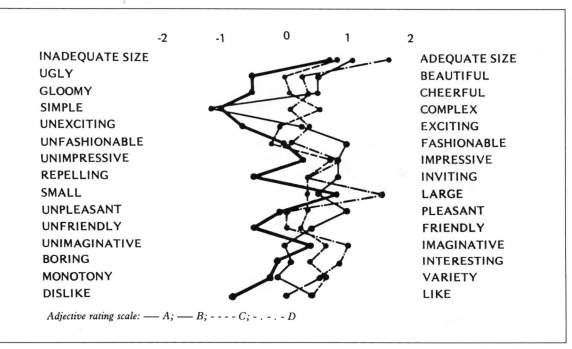

-2   -1   0   1   2

INADEQUATE SIZE	ADEQUATE SIZE
UGLY	BEAUTIFUL
GLOOMY	CHEERFUL
SIMPLE	COMPLEX
UNEXCITING	EXCITING
UNFASHIONABLE	FASHIONABLE
UNIMPRESSIVE	IMPRESSIVE
REPELLING	INVITING
SMALL	LARGE
UNPLEASANT	PLEASANT
UNFRIENDLY	FRIENDLY
UNIMAGINATIVE	IMAGINATIVE
BORING	INTERESTING
MONOTONY	VARIETY
DISLIKE	LIKE

Adjective rating scale: —— *A;* —— *B;* - - - - *C;* - . - . - *D*

Figure 2-12: Adjective rating scale comparing facades A, B, C, and D.

important, because arts council members were able to effectively engage in a discussion of the options available to them. The major limitation to this technique is the need for acceptance of the options presented by designers, since it is difficult to anticipate which option will be preferred by the participating residents.

Another technique that has been used to develop an understanding of people's environmental preferences is a questionnaire exploring variations in spatial character (Figure 2-13). Staff of the Durham Arts Council were asked to describe each of the photographs and to rate, in order of their preference, the photograph that best fit their idea of an arts center (Sanoff, 1983). Using the concept of personal constructs (Kelly, 1955), which relies on the people's ability to form independent judgments that contain polar opposites, staff carefully examined each of the pictures. The building featured in picture 4 was their first choice and was described as *interesting, attractive, inviting,* and *exciting.* Expressions of *modern, arty,* and *looks like it is designed for the arts* were used to further qualify that choice. Picture 3 was the second preference because the staff members believed that it successfully blended modern and classical features and appeared to belong to the community. The third choice was building 1 which presently houses the Durham Arts

7. Building Image – In the following section we are going to analyze different building facades with the purpose of defining the one that best suits the image of an arts center. Please, answer all following questions:	7.1. Please, number the pictures below in rank order, according to the image that best fits an art center.	7.2. Describe each of the five pictures.	7.3. What features do you particularly like in each of these five pictures?	7.4. What features do you particularly dislike in each of the five pictures?

Figure 2-13: Various art center building facades (Marilia DoVal & Henry Sanoff).

Council. Descriptions of *cold* and *traditional, too federal looking,* and *official* were the words used to characterize their present facility.

The exercise was especially illuminating since the council members initially believed that their building, the former city hall, was adequate in appearance. When comparing their facility with others that more effectively conveyed the image of an arts center, council members quickly altered their views about their facility and instructed the design team to explore modifications to their building that would be more expressive of an arts center.

As a result of the success of this comparison technique, three major art center spaces such as entrance lobby (Figure 2-14), an exhibition gallery, and an office, were selected for exploring differences in spatial character and sensitizing the participants to the range of possible options. The purpose of this exercise, however, was to provide a list of preselected adjective descriptors to expand the participants' vocabulary for distinguishing differences, since it was believed that the task required judgments that people were not accustomed to make.

In each case, a list of opposite pairs of adjectives was provided for staff ratings. Photographs were selected from a wide range of choices by judges with expertise in design. Criteria for the final selection of pictures were based on their representativeness of the different types within the spatial categories.

When rating exhibition gallery alternatives, the staff unanimously selected picture 5 (Figure 2-14) because it was *cheerful, inviting,* and *imaginative,* while picture 4 was unanimously classified as *cramped, gloomy,* and *unimaginative.* It is important to note that picture 4 represents their present facility. Again, juxtaposing the present situation with other places expressing different characteristics gave the participants a basis for a dialogue and critical assessment of the places they presently occupy. These studies imply that it is not only important to occupy old buildings, but that they may need to be modified to accommodate new uses as well as to convey a positive image that reflects their new use.

Using social science techniques such as the adjective rating scale or the semantic differential (Osgood, Suci, & Tannenbaum, 1957), in conjunction with photographic images, can promote an effective information exchange between designer and client/user. The choice of photographs clearly creates a "ceiling effect" in that it limits the respondents' choices. The photographic techniques included in the participatory process, used to complement surveys and spatial evaluations, were critical to the quality and acceptance of the final design solution. The focused format allowed client groups to progress beyond previous unsuccessful attempts to initiate a facility development project.

8. Visual Quality – The purpose of this section is to assess the adequacy of different settings to the performance of specific activities in the center.

    Three different activities were chosen.

    8.1. Entrance Lobby

a) List the picture numbers in rank order according to the image you have of an ideal lobby space.

    _____
    _____
    _____
    _____

b) Choose one adjective in each pair to describe each of these five pictures. Circle the picture number to show your choise.

EX:	1	2	3	4	5				1	2	3	4	5
	1	②	3	④	5	Ugly	Beautiful	①	2	③	4	⑤
	1	2	3	4	5	Cheerful	Gloomy	1	2	3	4	5
	1	2	3	4	5	Comfortable	Uncomfortable	1	2	3	4	5
	1	2	3	4	5	Dark	Light	1	2	3	4	5
	1	2	3	4	5	Imaginative	Unimaginative	1	2	3	4	5
	1	2	3	4	5	Inviting	Repelling	1	2	3	4	5
	1	2	3	4	5	Noisy	Quiet	1	2	3	4	5
	1	2	3	4	5	Spacious	Cramped	1	2	3	4	5
	1	2	3	4	5	Variety	Monotony	1	2	3	4	5

Figure 2-14: Options for an entrance lobby (Marilia DoVal & Henry Sanoff).

VISUAL APPRAISAL

Another approach for developing a deeper understanding of the visual environment is a self-guided tour. Unlike other assessment strategies that rely upon conventional social science techniques for describing and judging the environment, the checklist offers individuals and groups a procedure for taking a structured walk through a building. This is an impressionistic approach which increases people's awareness of the environment by focusing on visual factors. The results of such a walk-through encourage responses about views, walkways, barriers, daylight, orientation, wayfinding, and appearance.

The CRIG analysis, developed by Bishop (1977), allows observers to appraise visual quality in terms of four key elements—*context, routes, interface,* and *grouping.* Any building or group of buildings is amenable to such appraisal. By using a series of checklist questions and a numerical rating scheme, scores are assigned to the factor being appraised.

The process uses notes, drawings, and photographs to supplement the factors described in the checklist.

Numerical scores from 1 to 7 (1 = highly appropriate, 7 = highly inappropriate) are assigned to each question in the checklist. Individual scores are then averaged and an overall project score is assigned. An appraisal report would consider:

1. Description of the building(s) appraised with supportive illustrations (photographs, sketches, maps, diagrams).
2. Appraisal of the building(s) according to the four-factor analysis using the checklists, with responses and numerical scores for each question provided.
3. A paragraph describing the success or lack of success with which each factor is achieved or satisfied.
4. Analysis of numerical ratings by computation of average scores for each factor of the appraisal, and computation of the overall score for the building(s).
5. Concluding comments based upon the overall appraisal of the building(s).

Factor 1. CONTEXT: The building's setting

Highly appropriate   1 2 3 4 5 6 7   *Very inappropriate*   Score

1. How does the building suit the pattern of the surrounding streets?   _____

2. How does the scale of the building suit the site it sits upon?   _____

3. How does the scale of the building suit the scale of surrounding buildings?   _____

4. How does the scale suit the character of the neighborhood?   _____

5. Do the public and private areas relate well to one another?   _____

6. Do the land uses adjacent to the building seem to fit harmoniously with the building?   _____

7. Do the type of building and its intended use fit well with the type and uses of adjacent buildings?   _____

8. Does the appearance of the building fit well with the type of buildings surrounding it?   _____

9. Is the scale of the building suitable for its purpose on the site?   _____

Average Score (total/9) =

A summary paragraph should be written to express the observers' concerns about the way the building suits or fails to suit the context of the surrounding area. An example of such a summary is as follows:

> The site of the structure is the new Robson Square Complex located in the heart of downtown Vancouver. Four busy commercial streets—Howe, Smithe, Nelson and Hornby—surround the complex. A covered office walkway bridge connects the Law Courts to Robson Square by passing over Smithe Street.
>
> Instead of tall, narrow buildings rising vertically from the sidewalk, the architect has used an angled geometric structure for the building and has provided a considerable number of pedestrian walkways, grassy areas, trees, shrubs and water as well as seating areas. The Robson Square facility which connects to the Law Courts is a "people place" with gardens, private and public space, roller rinks, restaurants, an information center and a theatre complex. Other uses of surrounding land are mixed. The Law Courts are central to the city core with hotels, commercial office buildings, shops and restaurants located in buildings which are mostly in the 30-50 year age category and of mixed architctural features. Adjacent buildings such as the Hotel Vancouver and the old courthouse provide an interesting contrast with their unique and attractive architecture.
>
> The structure of the Law Court facility is so designed that different views of the surrounding building and of the structure itself are apparent from each level. The building, with its ample public space, allows access from adjacent streets and buildings and allows recreational and leisure time activity for the public as well as serving its intended function as a legal facility. (Davis, 1981)

Scores: (following completion of checklist on context) 4,2,1,1,2,2,3,2,2
Total = 19, Average = **2.1**

Factor 2. ROUTES: Routes are the traffic paths or passageways that allow the building to relate to its context

Highly appropriate   1 2 3 4 5 6 7   *Very inappropriate*   Score

1. Are sufficient routes, pathways, streets, and passageways provided to and around the building? _____

2. What are the flow patterns of traffic or people? Are there busy periods, quiet periods, one-way flows, regular movement patterns, traffic jams? Are the routes arranged to consider these factors? _____

3. Where are the nodes (meeting points) for traffic around the building and what happens there? _____

4. Do all the routes make sense? Are they understandable and convenient? _____

5. Are all the routes easily understood by newcomers, visitors,   _____
   service people?

6. How well are the routes marked? Are the markings clear   _____
   and easily understood?

7. How effectively do the routes link the building to the sur-   _____
   rounding buildings or structures?

                                    Average Score (total/7) =

A summary paragraph should be written to describe the way in which
the routes in and around the building(s) relate the building to its
context and the success with which the routes accomplish that purpose.

**Factor 3. INTERFACE: A building is essentially an enclosure that
separates an interior private space from exterior public space. The
interface is the crucial meeting place where the inside of the
building connects with the outside. (Figure 2-15)**

Figure 2-15: Connections to outdoors: University of Sydney, School of Architecture
(Photo: Henry Sanoff). *Interface:* There are a number of entrances at different street
levels of the architecture school. Use of large glass areas provides ample light at
entrances and corridors. The function of the building is apparent from its outside
appearance. Although there are no signs informing visitors about the building's
function, the large glass areas suggest the presence of studios. *Score: (from completion
of interface checklist)* 5,2,2,3,2,1,4,3, = 23/8 = 2.9

Highly appropriate   1 2 3 4 5 6 7   *Very inappropriate*   Score

1. How clearly or effectively does the exterior of the building   _____
   indicate its interior function(s)?

2. How effectively does the exterior of the building connect   _____
   with the outside of the building? Are the connections appropriate and functional?

3. Are the exits and entrances easily accessible?   _____

4. Are the various openings related to thoughtful planning of   _____
   the interior? (Consider entry of light, view, privacy, noise,
   heat, glare, atmosphere, etc.)

5. Are the exitways appropriate from a safety point of view?   _____

6. When you move from the exterior of the building to the   _____
   interior by means of the main entrance, is the experience
   pleasant, interesting, or special in any way?

7. Are the clues to what is public and what is private space   _____
   clear to the visitor?

8. Have the designers, in your opinion, handled the problem   _____
   of interface well in their design of this building?

                                   Average Score (total/8) =

A summary paragraph should be written describing how well the design of the building has addressed the problem of interface, including
the strengths and weaknesses of the design, and how it might be improved.

**Factor 4. GROUPING: Buildings are usually divided into sections
which are organized in form into some type of grouping. Grouping
of the parts gives both form and meaning as well as variety to the
building. (Figure 2-16)**

Highly appropriate   1 2 3 4 5 6 7   *Very inappropriate*   Score

1. Concentrate on the subdivision of the building's parts as   _____
   viewed from the outside. What parts are evident? Do the
   parts integrate well with each other and form an effective
   and pleasing appearance?

2. Do the subdivided parts of the building appear to have a   _____
   specific function? Is the function of each part easy to identify?

Figure 2-16: Massing of building elements: University of Sydney, School of Architecture (Photo: Henry Sanoff). *Groupings:* Viewed from the campus entrance, the architecture school creates an intersecting massing of building elements. From the city street, the visitor enters through a door into a walled court, providing a different face to the street than to the campus. Circulation within the building is interrupted by a two-story space which redirects movement through studio areas.

3. Is it clear what various subdivisions of the building might _____ mean to visitors? Would a visitor know where to go on entering the building?

4. Are the various parts of the building planned carefully in _____ relation to one another and to the characteristics of the site?

5. Is there sufficient relationship between the parts of the _____ building for it to appear as one unified structure?

6. Does enough variation exist in the structural parts and _____ groupings to provide interest and variety?

Average Score (total/6) =

A summary paragraph should be written to discuss the building's subdivision into identifiable parts, the way those parts are grouped, and how successfully the concept of grouping was employed.

Finally, a synopsis of the assessment might be:

An extremely interesting structure that combines public space and interest with an important community and government function in a unique and creative way. To the visitor, function and routes of access may be somewhat obscure, however the uniqueness and versatility of the design, which is appealing, prove to be a significant factor in the apraisal (Davis, p. 37).

APPROACH ROAD PLANTING

In a study of country towns and street planting in Australia, Armstrong and Burton (1986) sought to interpret the form of towns with particular reference to public plantings. Although they recognized that each place has its own uniqueness, their study concentrated on the use of plant materials and how they may or may not reinforce the natural or cultural elements of a particular place. The town layout comprised a number of town elements. These elements were approach roads, the town edges, transportation links, the residential, commercial, and industrial areas, as well as the detailed elements of important buildings and places. As this study was concerned with street and roadside planting, the town elements were best considered in terms of movement into and through the town, and among those pathways identified as linkages between elements.

The first element of a town which is experienced is the approach road. In New South Wales the indigenous trees that mark the town entrance vary from the coastal setting, to the western plains, or within the undulating hills. Approach roads are usually planted with roadside trees, which may be in formal rows or remnant indigenous trees left as the town entrance. Where continuous development has occurred, old approach road plantings can become incorporated into the town fabric. More frequently, a town is visually isolated and the approach road marks the entrance to a town. Each of the different approach road plantings creates a particular character which is culturally significant in its regional setting. In some cases the approach road planting is the same as other planted elements in the landscape, such as the sugar gum avenues in the Riverina which are also windbreaks in the fields. In other cases, the approach road planting is continued into the town so that arrival within the town fabric is not clearly distinguished. The significance of this character is best understood through the perceptions of the town residents. This is particularly important since many of the towns are undergoing development changes that may inadvertently alter the character of the town. These changes often occur without any prior knowledge by the town residents.

In an effort to conduct a representative study of approach road planting, Armstrong and Burton sampled a number of towns located in various regions of the state. They photographed the approach road and main street of each town and developed a survey instrument (Figure 2-17) to be used in conjunction with any proposed town changes.

(Facing page)
Figure 2-17: Small town approach roads in Australia (Photo: Helen Armstrong).

They also analyzed the planting variations that occurred in the different regions. Approach road plantings in treeless settings, they observed, were a strong cultural feature. In some cases the approach road planting continued as street planting within the town. Other towns were characterized by a mixture of species. In some instances, particularly in the approach to mountain towns, trees were used as windbreaks outside the town.

The photoquestionnaire proposes to address two issues: residents' perception of the town character and of the main street. The street tree survey has been completed. The next phase will focus on residents' perceptions. The study is particularly timely since many country towns in Australia are experiencing growth and development changes.

SIGNSCAPE

Signage, the use of signs, exists for the purpose of conveying information to people passing by, whether pedestrians or motorists. The signscape is an aggregation of symbols and letters as they appear on signs, billboards, storefronts, marquees, canopies, and all other visual media located on buildings. The impact of signscape is significant since previous research involving the public's response (Nasar, 1988) has shown that visual quality in a community can be greatly reduced by the appearance of signs and billboards.

In a study of perceived visual quality, Nasar (1988) examined the effects of complexity and coherence in emotional judgments associated with environmental evaluation. The choice of complexity and coherence as critical factors was based on the work of Berlyne (1972) and Wohlwhill (1976) in which connections between pleasantness and arousal influenced judgments of environments described as pleasant. The environment must be involving to attract human attention, and it must make sense for humans to operate in it. Thus, complexity and coherence are integrally related in satisfying human needs.

Evaluation studies were conducted with shoppers and merchants by using a scale model of a commercial strip which was constructed and photographed with nine different signscapes ranging in degrees of complexity and contrast. Nasar defined *complexity* as scene variation, and *coherence* as scene legibility. Complexity was altered through variation among the signs in terms of location, shape, color, direction, and lettering style.

The least complex signage (Figure 2-18) consisted of signs of uniform shape, color, and lettering style mounted in the same location and direction. The most complex (Figure 2-19) had signs differing in all characteristics. The moderately complex situation (Figure 2-20)

Figure 2-18: Signage in commercial strips. (a) Least complex; most coherent. (b) Least complex; moderately coherent. (c) Least complex; least coherent. (Photos: Jack Nasar).

a

b

c

Figure 2-19: Signage in commercial strips. (a) Moderately complex; most coherent. (b) Moderately complex; moderately coherent. (c) Moderately complex; least coherent (Photos: Jack Nasar).

a

b

c

Figure 2-20: Signage in commercial strips. (a) Most complex; least coherent. (b) Most complex; moderately coherent. (c) Most complex; most coherent. (Photos: Jack Nasar).

67

contained some variety in signage. Contrast (noncoherence) was intro-duced by manipulating variables within each sign: size and lettering style, and contrast of color and material of the sign and lettering in relation to the background. The signscape with the least contrast had the smallest signs and letters in natural colors. The signscape with the greatest contrast had the largest signs and letters, brightest colors, and highest color contrast between letters and background. The moderate contrast signscape had middle-sized signs and letters and less intense color.

Photographs of nine different conditions of complexity and contrast were produced by combining the factors. Participants in the study were asked to rank order the nine scenes for coherence, from the most to the least coherent. The results indicated that the most coherent signscape was the least complex and the least contrasting. The findings also suggested that signscape complexity reduced coherence, but at high levels of complexity there was no perceived difference in levels of contrast.

A larger sample of shoppers and merchants was used for a follow-up study where each respondent ranked the nine photographs in terms of pleasantness, excitement, and calmness, three of the most salient aspects of environmental evaluation (Ward & Russell, 1981). The intent here was to discover what influence complexity and coher-ence might have on scene evaluation. The results indicated that mer-chants and shoppers, alike, responded most favorably to a moderately complex and highly coherent retail strip (Figure 2-20).

Based on the results of the studies, Nasar evaluated sign regulations in the commercial district of the study area. When he discovered that the results did not produce the desired effect of moderate complexity and high coherence in the real environment, he suggested changes in local standards. Having demonstrated that emotional judgments can be altered by varying physical conditions, Nasar pointed to the possi-bility of meeting goals other than perceived pleasantness—for exam-ple, achieving high excitement in a major entertainment area. Overall, the principle of the dependence of aesthetic value on "unity in variety" can be used by planners and designers to improve the perceived visual quality of the signscape and the city.

STREETSCAPE GRAPHICS

Street graphics pertain to symbols and letters as they appear on signs, billboards, storefronts, marquees, canopies, and other visual media located on buildings. Of all the design elements in a streetscape, signs have the strongest impact. An effective sign communicates a message.

Signs supply information, therefore their location and size contribute to their communication capability. Wall signs can be most effective when they are designed to fit the buildings on which they are mounted. The information content of the sign can vary. While some messages are better conveyed by abstract symbols or pictures, most signs require verbal messages. The lettering on signs and buildings should consider legibility, readability, and compatibility. The choice of type style and word spacing will influence legibility and readability.

A graphic design approach was developed to assist communities in creating and evaluating signscapes. A kit of materials was developed to enable decisions about *best sign location, sign shape, sign graphics,* and *lettering style.* A facade base sheet (Figure 2-21) was prepared with an overlay grid (Figure 2-22) to aid in determining the best sign location. A type sample sheet (Figure 2-23) included alternative shapes, sizes, and type lettering styles to be affixed to the facade base sheet (Figure 2-24)

STREETSCAPE WORKSHOP

Following the hypothetical exercise that emphasizes streetscape graphics, community members would be more knowledgeable and amenable to discussions about their own street improvements. Relying on the graphic principles developed in the previous exercise, design proposals would be generated and compared to drawings of the present streetscape (Figure 2-25). This method is most effective with many small groups where community participants make and defend personal choices as they seek group consensus. Comparisons between groups can generate a variety of likes and dislikes. This feedback would enable designers to proceed effectively to the next stage of design development with solutions that are within the range of acceptability.

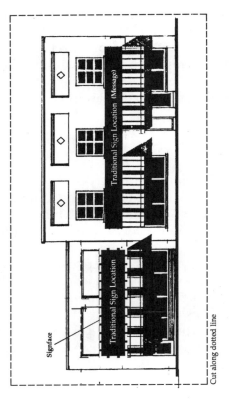

The term **Signface** refers to the surface on which the **Message** is placed.

Note Message

The term **Message** (Traditional Sign Location) shown on the illustrated Building Facade, refers to all items on signface; i.e. letters, arrows, symbols, lines, etc.

Graphic Design Approach

Visualize how your sign will appear in relation to the entire facade.

Consider the facade as a second background.

Gridlines follow natural lines of facade to help organize information.

The Building Facade Base Sheet is provided as an Underlay for the Grid Overlay (see Grid Overlay).

Figure 2-21: Building facade base sheet (Robert Kreda).

This excercise will give the particpants the opportunity to examine the sign options available by using the cut-out overlay grid as a design tool in order to determine the best sign location.

The Grid

The grid may take on many forms. It may define the margins and type columns or it may provide a framework for a wide range of typographic options and visual opportunities.

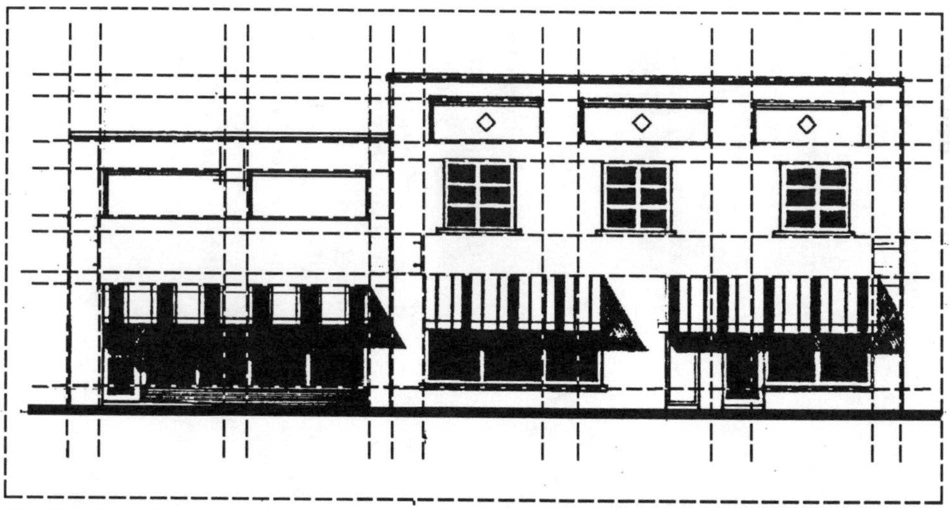

Figure 2-22: Building facade and grid overlay (Robert Kreda).

The pattern of a grid is guided by the function of the content and the design concept.

Each grid is custom-made to fit the requirements of a specific project.

The grid is the visual organizing structure for all worded messages.

Building Facade Sign Application

This activity gives the participant, the opportunity to investigate the following:

- best sign location
- sign shape
- sign graphics
- lettering style

Instructions

Cut-Out Sign Type sample and place into desired position on Building Facade plate as provided.

The Sign Element should do the following:

- be readable
- be in harmony with the building
- be appropriate
- be aesthetically pleasing
- be legible
- be in scale with the building

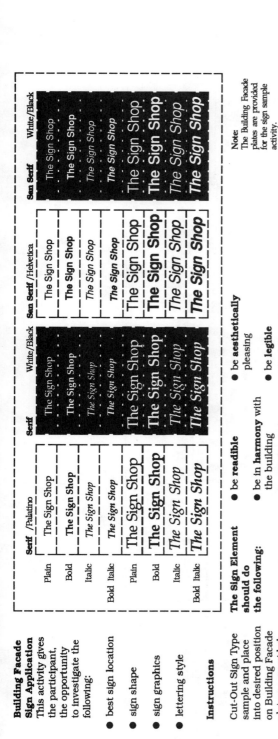

	Serif / Palatino	White/Black	San Serif / Helvetica	White/Black
Plain	The Sign Shop	The Sign Shop	The Sign Shop	The Sign Shop
Bold	**The Sign Shop**	**The Sign Shop**	**The Sign Shop**	**The Sign Shop**
Italic	*The Sign Shop*	*The Sign Shop*	*The Sign Shop*	*The Sign Shop*
Bold Italic	***The Sign Shop***	***The Sign Shop***	***The Sign Shop***	***The Sign Shop***

Note:
The Building Facade plates are provided for the sign sample activity.

Figure 2-23: Sign samples (Robert Kreda).

Environmental Graphics can:

- break monotony
- add color and spirit
- impart a sense of identity
- move the viewer through and around
- create a sense of drama
- improve visual linkages

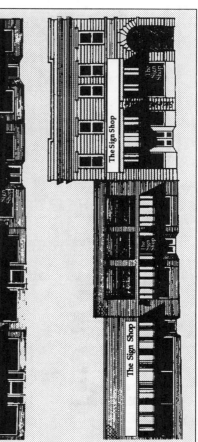

Figure 2-24: Town appearance (Robert Kreda).

Quite often the visual appearance of a town is difficult to assess. Many of the factors influential in the appearance of a town are not easily quantified and as a result are difficult to agree upon.

In an effort to adequately discuss the character of a town, it is necessary to identify the salient features that affect its appearance.

The presence of "image" products, such as signs, can have either a positive or a negative influence.

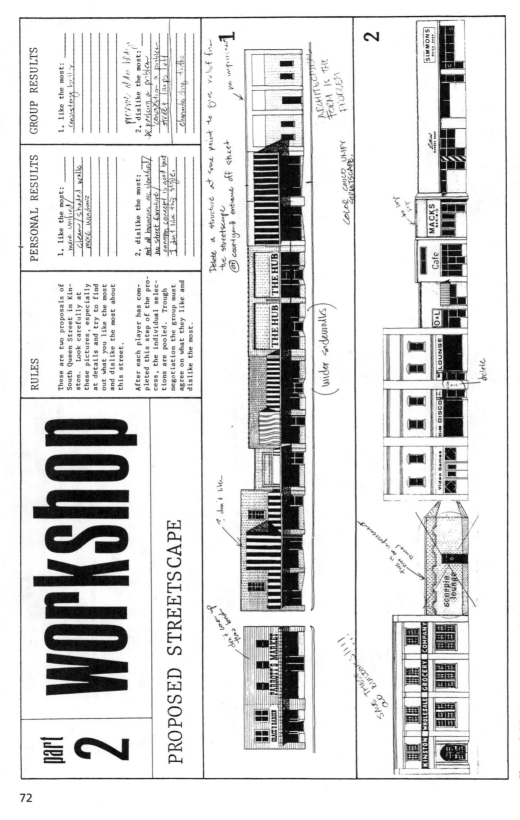

part 2
workshop

PROPOSED STREETSCAPE

RULES	PERSONAL RESULTS	GROUP RESULTS
These are two proposals of South Queen Street in Kinston. Look carefully at these pictures, especially at details and try to find out what you like the most and dislike the most about this street.	1. like the most: _____ more unified/ clean/ shaded walks more windows	1. like the most: _____ consistency / utility
After each player has completed this step of the process, the individual selections are pooled. Trough negotiation the group must agree on what they like and dislike the most.	2. dislike the most: _____ not all buildings are unified/ no street furniture/ canopy concept is good but I don't like this style.	2. dislike the most: _____ ✗ perhaps a problem congestion a problem street lamps off climate dog traffic

1

Delete a structure at some point to give relief from the streetscape
@ courtyard entrance off street

no improvement

ARCHITECTURAL FORM IS THE PROBLEM

COLOR COULD UNIFY STREETSCAPE.

(wider sidewalks)

? don't like

don't wrap up

THE HUB   THE HUB

DM DISCO   LOUNGE   O&L   Video Games

delete

georgia lounge

this is out of proportion

KINSTON WHOLESALE GROCERY COMPANY

SAVE THESE 2 BUILDINGS!!!

2

SIMMONS

MACKS   Cafe

PARROTT'S MARKET

Figure 2-25: Streetscape workshop results.

3

ENVIRONMENTAL MAPPING

The feeling of orientation is essential to our well-being within the environment. Basically, it allows us to know where we are, to have a sense of where to go next, and to be able to choose an adequate route to get there. In addition to allowing us to so navigate, knowing our relative position in a place gives us a sense of ease and enjoyment and allows us to appreciate new and unexpected features.

On a survival level, as Lozano (1988) has pointed out, orientation allows us to cope with personal threat, sorting out minimum risk paths, exiting highways safely at high speeds, and finding essential goods and services. It involves a level of differentiation, or variety, in the environment to provide clues to direction, distances, and changes, as well as a sense of familarity within it. Lack of orientation, on the other hand, can result from introduction of too much variety without perceived links, or too little variety, producing an unstimulating, monotonous backdrop. Hall (1966) considered the serious effects of sensory deprivation—loss of contact with reality, and hallucination—resulting from lack of "body feedback." The sense of orientation, and the cues for establishing it, should be a shared part of a culture, accessible to those who have experienced similar kinds of environments.

The most ancient means of orientation is sun movement. However, we usually make use of other points of reference to locate ourselves, especially in an urban area. Sometimes our reference is a building that stands out from its neighbors, at other times it is a distinctly arborized avenue, or even a park within a built neighborhood. Even with no prior direct contact with a particular place, the shared systems of orientation within our culture offer us clues for establishing locations. In any case, there is usually a prominent point or location or identifying element to which we can refer to find our way within our surroundings. Visual access, or the ability to differentiate environmental features, is a factor that influences people's spatial orientation (Gärling, Book, & Lindberg, 1986).

Orientation also involves a sense of position in time. The time of the day can be sensed through changes in light and shade on a building or street. The different periods of the year produce changes in the landscape as well, causing an area to take on different appearances with the seasons. Longer historical periods can normally be identified through changes in the visual characteristics of the environment.

Modifications in the physical characteristics of our surroundings can strongly affect our sense of orientation: demolition of buildings, or changes in the system of paths, can sometimes deprive us of important reference points, without which finding our way becomes impossible.

COGNITIVE MAPPING

Various philosophies of the subject–object relationship range from the belief that knowledge of the world is innate to humans (a priori), to the belief that all knowledge of reality comes from our sensory data (a posteriori). Somewhere between these extremes lies the belief that knowledge is a construction of thought, or a synthesis of the "matter" of experience and the "form" which the understanding imposes upon it.

These internal constructions arise from a developmental process encompassing all aspects of our lives, and they form the basis of our beliefs about and actions in the world. Boulding (1964) calls this important mental construct the *image,* and argues that it is the basis for all action when he writes, "the act depends on the whole cognitive-valuation structure, that is, on the image."

Although the image is important to all ways of existing in the world, the images which people hold of their physical environment are the ones which are most important to environmental designers and researchers. By understanding how our physical surroundings affect us and our behavior, we may become more aware, and therefore more in control of ourselves and our environments. This motivation, ultimately political, is the justification for inquiry into mental imagery of the built environment. "Implicit . . . is the belief that by discovering individual and group perceptions, processing them, and communicating results, some improvement in man's lot will be achieved" (Goodey, 1974, p. 36).

The question which concerns us regarding mental imagery is this: is it possible to know what a person's internal constructions about the environment actually are, and if so, how? Environmental designers and researchers are interested in eliciting these constructions as objectively as possible, with the ultimate goal of influencing them. Since cognitive representations "must be inferred from one or more external, symbolic representations or from other forms of observable behavior" (Moore & Golledge, 1976, p. 8), difficult methodological questions arise as to how to get at the information inside people's heads.

There are two prominent methodological problems, each of which applies to a broad category of experimentation. *Observation* is one such category, which might include verbal responses to questionnaires as well as "tracking people through known and unknown environments and observing their responses" (Golledge, 1976, p. 302). Questionnaires present a difficulty in that they may influence responses by asking particular questions instead of possible others, and they necessarily phrase questions in particular ways. In fact, any attempt at eliciting information by providing the subject with some sort of stimulus or cue (whether verbal or not) is plagued by this problem. In an experiment designed to examine student perceptions of the locations of American cities relative to Grand Forks, North Dakota, Goodey (1974) states that "the supposedly neutral techniques such as providing the subjects with some sort of stimulus or cue for eliciting perceptions of location may bias information recorded to the exclusion of much knowledge which the respondent can offer given the appropriate cue." The positive side of this problem is that the researcher may stimulate otherwise dominant interest in and awareness of the environment.

The dilemma also exists with visual methods of observation such as photo interviewing, though perhaps to a lesser extent. Collier (1979) indicates that photographs are precise records of material reality; however, the visual code must be broken if the camera is to make any real contribution to anthropological understanding. The information locked in visual content must then be transformed by the observer into a useful, analyzable form.

A second broad category of extracting cognitive information is to ask the subject to record *self-reports* about the environment, either while experiencing it or while recording it. The form of these reports may vary: they may be verbal, written, or visual (in the form of sketches or models). The conclusion researchers draw from such a report is that only the information included in the report has some significance for the subject.

The problem with self-reports is that they call on skills of the subject which may be developed to varying degrees in different people. Not only may they require memory skills, but they also may require graphic or cartographic skills as well. In general, maps generated in these experiments yield topological information such as proximity, enclosure, order, and sequence, and do not yield any kind of veridical metric information. In fact, considerable doubt has been placed on the value of trying to extract metric and geometric information from sketched material (Golledge, 1976, p. 311).

Downs and Stea (1977) define cognitive mapping as "a process composed of a series of psychological transformations by which an individual acquires, codes, recalls, and decodes information about the relative locations and attributes of phenomena in his everyday spatial environment" (p. 9). They go on to assert that the cognitive map determines an individual's spatial behavior. Boulding (1964) expands upon this point to include more than just spatial behavior when he writes that "the act depends on the whole cognitive valuation structure." Passini (1984, p. 46) adds a link between cognitive mapping or "information-generating ability that allows us to understand the world around us . . . and a decision-executing ability that transforms decisions into behavioral actions." He proposes a planning or decision-making process as the link between image and behavior.

A cognitive map is not necessarily a "map," but a "functional analogue" (Downs & Stea, 1977, pp. 11–12). That is, the cognitive map functions like a cartographic map in that both involve the encoding and decoding of spatial information. Both involve a "transformation of information about spatial phenomena from one set of absolute space relationships into a set which is adaptive or useful in terms of human spatial behavior" (p. 12).

Understanding this transformation of spatial information from image into behavior is at the heart of environmental perception research. Again, getting at the information inside people's heads is the challenge, since perception of an environment can be measured in a number of ways. One technique is to ask a sample of people how they feel about an environment and its important attributes. This technique relies heavily on individuals' explanations of what they perceive. Another more indirect method assumes an intrinsic relationship between people's behavior patterns and what they perceive in an environment. By mapping the activity patterns of a sample of households, we can describe their ecological neighborhood.

The type of environmental knowledge contained in cognitive maps has been the subject of considerable study (Golledge, 1987). There is, however, agreement that there is a distinction between knowledge about places and about spatial relationships. Spatial knowledge consists of knowledge of routes and of the locations of key environmental features. Therefore, a cognitive map is a mental construct that directs the selection of immediately available information in the environment (Neisser, 1976). A cognitive map influences and is influenced by the information in the environment. Thus, there is a mutual dependency between direct perception of the properties of the environment and the cognitive map of the environment which cannot be directly perceived. Cognitive maps are acquired predominantly through the direct experience of walking from one place to another. A resulting knowledge is gained about spatial relationships, places, and about where spatial knowledge consists of knowing routes and locations of important places. A cognitive map, then, is related to spatial orientation, navigation, and recognition.

Cognitive maps of cities differ from cognitive maps of smaller scale environments. These maps are acquired under conditions of travel, in which verbal and printed communications may be as important as direct experience. Canter (1977), for example, showed that the characteristics of London subway maps influenced travelers' cognitive map of the city. Cognitive maps of cities contain standardized conceptual elements like landmarks, nodes, paths, districts, and edges (Lynch, 1960), which vary in their specificity or abstraction. Briefly, the way in which cognitive maps of the environment are represented will vary with different spatial scales.

DIRECT OBSERVATION

Observation and behavioral mapping is a method for describing what people do in the designed environment. It is an indirect approach compared to the methods that have relied on direct user involvement in seeking design-related information. Direct participation sees the users as "subjects" who have something to say about their environmental preferences and actions; this alternative approach views people as "objects" and observes their periodic behavior as a basis for making design decisions (Canter, 1970).

Behavioral observation is a valuable tool of the social sciences, which has established its validity as a supplement to direct methods of study and measurement. Erroneous conclusions have been drawn from exclusive use of interviews and questionnaires in assessing human behavior. Such techniques are foreign intrusions into the situation under study, often eliciting atypical responses from a limited or special subset of participants. Those questioned must be accessible to the investigator and willing to cooperate; moreover, their responses must be assumed to be relatively unbiased if not deliberately perverse. In large studies, the investigator must often resort to random sampling of subjects, which may overlook or underrate significant types of responses. Direct observation, on the other hand, takes its information from the uninterrupted activity of the participants who are usually unaware that they are supplying it.

In addition to the immediate and obvious technique of observing behavior in progress, observation methods can include studying physical evidence left by the interaction of people and the environment (Sanoff & Coates, 1971). Of particular use to the designer who seeks to understand the ways in which people use their play and work places are the phenomena of erosion and accretion. In a museum, for instance, the glass cases surrounding exhibits that are viewed by the most people will accrue a greater number of hand or nose prints, or floor tiles may be eroded more quickly and require more frequent replacement (Webb et al., 1972). Dust collection on library books can be an indication of nonpopularity of the collection or nonuse of a particular area, while dirty edges, smudges, finger marks, and underlining on pages can indicate the reverse (Webb et al., 1972). Broken windows and litter may indicate indifference to or abuse of an environment, and numbers and types of locks suggest fears about security (Friedman, Zimring, & Zube, 1978).

Psychologists Ittleson, Proshansky & Rirlin (1970) observed and recorded the activities of patients in hospital rooms. Comparing the sociability of patients in single rooms, double rooms, and wards, they found that when the number of patients in a room is smaller, social activity is greater. By observing unobtrusively, designers can learn what people do in the environment without influencing their actions. This method of looking at action between people and their environments has added value when users are unable to evaluate their surroundings and communicate their reactions. The word "environment" might include everything except the people themselves; the environment can be a complete building, part of a building, or an outdoor area.

People may modify their actions when they realize they are being watched, but since observation cuts a window in settings where people's behavior normally occurs, they may not realize or be concerned that they are being observed. Hidden observation is most often used in public places and is appropriate as long as anonymity of subjects is preserved. In some environments observers may take part in activities rather than hide. The technique of participant observation, which is the principal information-gathering technique in anthropology (Jacobs, 1970), is used by a single observer who becomes a member of the group. Every aspect of the culture is observed and recorded, following the entire group rather than the behavior of an individual. Since it is difficult for one observer to participate in all roles in a group, observation may be biased by the viewpoints obtained. In a hospital, for instance, where the staff is large and patients are admitted and discharged daily, an observer walking in the hallway may not be noticed. Bechtel (1965) points out, however, that a particpant observer in a mental hospital would respond differently depending on whether the observer was posing as a patient or an attendant. These approaches tend to be impressionistic, and are most appropriate for problem definition (Bechtel & Zeisel, 1987).

Valuable information may be obtained when behavior is systematically recorded. Casual observation may result in incomplete findings that reveal only what seems to be obvious. Carefully planned observation enables designers to collect and use accurately all the pieces of information that describe human behavior. In order to observe systematically, four basic components should be considered.

What may one need to know about people? Important information could include the number of persons, the amount of time each is observed, the sex, age, and exact location of each person, and whether or not people are collected in groups.

What might one need to know about activities? Activities will be the things people are doing, the defined, physical interactions between a person and an environmental cue. Having been designed to support specific activities, cues will tell people what activities should occur in a space.

What might one need to know about the setting? Cues should define settings where activity or groups of activities should occur. One may think of buildings as groups of rooms with physical boundaries: the ceiling, the floor, and the walls. Each room may support one or more activities. A classroom may have such activity centers as those for science, math, reading, and art. A hospital foyer may have settings for visiting, admitting patients, discharging patients, and giving out information.

What will one need to know about timing? Each setting might be observed a number of times. Settings can be observed at specific time intervals, such as every five minutes or every hour. The length of the time interval will depend on how the activity schedule of the building affects people's behavior. Observations may not be relevant during special times such as holidays because behavior may change. Observation should take place during a complete time cycle, a time period during which all activities occur. The cycle may be the five-day working week, or it may include the weekend if the building is in use seven days a week. The time cycle may include several weeks, months, or seasons.

In planning an observational study, decisions need to be made about the type of study desirable. Comparisons of different types of workplaces planned for the same activities can be made. The Ittleson,

Proshansky & Rivlin study (1970) for example, compared the social activities of hospital patients who stayed in single rooms, double rooms, and wards with several beds. After the nature of the study has been determined, relevant observations and recordings can be made according to each of the four component variables.

A data form can be designed to record information quickly and clearly. There might be places for the date, day of the week, time of day, and weather conditions. The data sheet may have a place for each setting that will be observed, including blanks for such typical settings as entrance lobby, main lounge, and elevator area. These will be places to record facts about people in each setting. If appropriate, enough copies of the data sheet may be produced so that a new one can be used for each observation.

To illustrate how people use spaces, behavioral maps of the setting can be drawn (see Figure 3-1). In making a behavioral map, a floor plan of the building or a site plan of an outdoor space should be drawn. Numbers and behavior of people can be indicated in each setting, suggesting the influence of cues such as furniture and equipment. By noting the locations and activities of people, conflicts in a

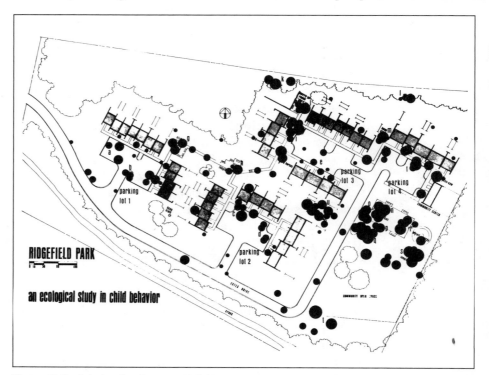

Figure 3-1: A behavioral map: Children's activities located on a site plan (Drawing: Henry Sanoff).

setting can be determined. A behavioral map may be used to compare the number of people using a space with the number of people the space was designed for.

When data forms and plans have been prepared, data can be collected by moving from setting to setting until each has been observed the desired number of times. The simple act of observation will suggest ways the data can be used. For behavioral maps, observations can be compiled onto one plan to see how people use each space. By comparing maps of different time periods, patterns of spatial uses can be studied. Using information on the data sheets, comparative charts can be constructed. A chart, based on the data sheets, may compare the number of people or activities in each space over a period of time. Comparisons can also be made between the number of people with different activities in each setting and the number of activities which actually occur in the designed settings.

There may be other questions that need to be asked when observing behavioral settings. Bechtel (1977) suggests the following:

> To what extent does it appear that friendly informal communication is occurring?
> Are different types of users segregated into groups?
> Is the setting centrally located? Is it readily accessible to all groups it should serve? Explain.
> Is the setting free from visual boundaries that might obscure it from people who pass by? Is it open on one or more sides? Is the arrangement such that people can face one another while seated? Can people see nearby traffic from their seats? Explain.

Considering the character and causal factors associated with activities will allow designers to see patterns of movement as the result of environmental successes and failures.

OBSERVING LIBRARY VISITORS

By unobtrusively observing patrons using a downtown library, a team of three observers was able to summarize the behavioral actions of visitors to the main and lower levels during two successive days.

Observers were stationed at fixed locations, systematically recording the patrons, their age and sex, and the patterns of their activities on each level. Visitors could enter the library from two opposite sides, the primary one along a pedestrian mall. Observations indicated that the entrances were equally used, although business people and shoppers tended to use the mall entrance.

Once entering the library, the majority of patrons were sufficiently familiar with the layout that they proceeded directly to their initial destination: the magazine area on the street level or the reference–study area on the level below. The main level contained mostly browsers who looked at the exhibits, book sales, and novels. Their visits tended to be twenty minutes in duration. The majority of the pat: ons were in the newspaper and magazine area, while others were m(andering.

Those patrons using the lower reference area were divided into four major user types: people using microfilm, people studying, péople using the reference area, and people in the stacks searching for a book. The majority of the users on the reference level were teenagers and college students. While these patrons would rarely check out a book, they would often browse through the magazine area before departing.

In addition to the visitor flow through the library, other information was obtained pertaining to satisfaction with comfort and illumination levels in all the occupied areas. The findings indicated that many work and storage areas requiring highly controlled light and temperature levels were not satisfactory in the present building. (Library materials can rapidly deteriorate when they are exposed to daylight and excessive humidity).

Individual comfort, too, was difficult to achieve since the heating and cooling system was not responsive to the variations in human tasks and their requirements. Similarly, a uniform illumination system did not provide the appropriate levels for different tasks, as reported by the building occupants.

A considerable amount of observable information can be recorded through behavioral surveys. In this study, an activity setting data sheet was constructed to record desirable characteristics based on repeated observations of the present setting.

MAPPING SCHOOLS

To supplement information about the flow patterns of people using a high school campus, a series of real time studies was conducted to understand how students, teachers, and staff use the environment and how they feel about their place in it. Techniques such as cognitive maps and tracking studies provide useful insights into how a campus is used. A cognitive map can show which street and building features are recalled about the campus (Kaplan, 1973). The value of using a map is based on the belief that people store information about their environment in simplified form and in relation to other information they already have. It further assumes that this information is coded in a structure which people carry in their head, and that this structure corresponds to the environment it represents. Maps are an indicator of important environmental features that need to be considered when site and building modifications are proposed.

Different student classes were requested to draw maps of their campus as well as drawings of their image of the "main" building. While there was no commonly agreed upon reference to a main building on this high school campus, students' perceptions were sought of the most significant campus building. The maps described the level of student comprehension of the campus while drawings of the buildings conveyed key architectural features, which when combined, provided insights into the importance students attribute to particular environmental features. The results were revealing, since all students made drawings of the original campus building which is currently on the National Register of Historic Places. When comparing the building features depicted on the drawings with the actual building, it was evident that the students accurately located the entrance and tower on their drawings, though few indicated building materials. Most had carefully located the clock in the tower, frequently larger than the windows (Figure 3-2), while very few drawings were proportionally accurate or indicated the building's edges. Plan drawings, however, consistently represented the buildings' basic form which was articulated by the auditorium, the girls gym, and the interior courtyard. The image of the high school was embodied in the historic building, which has been the subject of modification for many years. For many students the building and its tower symbolized the high school campus, which is an aggregation of numerous additions and extensions to the original building.

Although the campus map drawings revealed major circulation paths and the location of open spaces, more specific data on circulation paths were obtained through tracking studies of staff and students during key hours of the day. By stationing observers at various locations on campus, all staff and student movements were recorded at specific time intervals and subsequently transcribed onto a series of composite maps describing traffic patterns and their frequency (Figure 3-3).

In addition, activity logs or diaries, which combine the best features of observation and questionnaire techniques, were kept by a number of students. Self-observation recordings such as a diary, where events are logged at specific time intervals, provided a dynamic picture of the environment's use over time. Student self-observation reports provided a clearer picture of relations between user activity and the corresponding campus locations than more conventional observation methods. Although preliminary field observation and interviews had

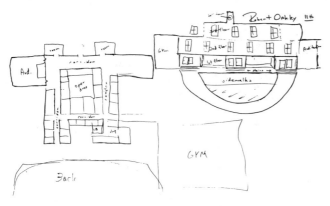

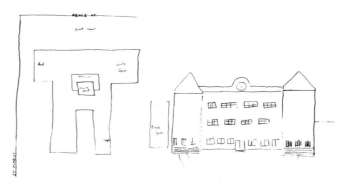

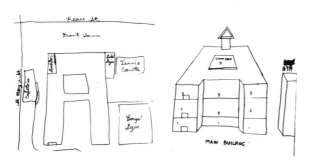

Figure 3-2: Students' drawings of the main campus building (Drawing: Tun Sing Chen & Henry Sanoff).

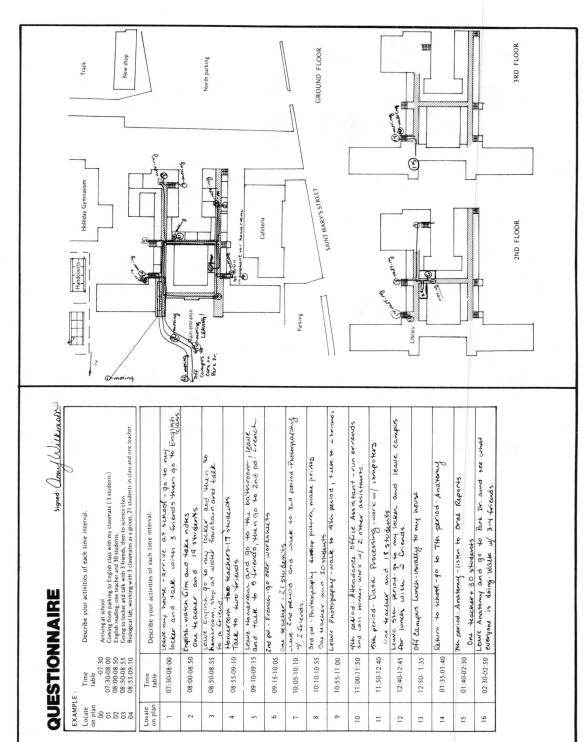

QUESTIONNAIRE

Signed: Amy Wilkinson

EXAMPLE:

Locate on plan	Time table	Describe your activities of each time interval.
00	—07:30	Arriving at school
01	07:30–08:00	Coming from parking to English class with my classmate (3 students)
02	08:00–08:50	English reading, one teacher and 30 students.
03	08:50–08:55	Going to locker and talk with 3 friends, then to science class
04	08:55–09:10	Biological lab, working with 3 classmates as a group, 21 students in class and one teacher.

Locate on plan	Time table	Describe your activities of each time interval.
1	07:30–08:00	Leave my home - arrive at school - go to my locker and talk with 3 friends then go to English class.
2	08:00–08:50	English - watch film and take notes. One teacher and 14 students
3	08:50–08:55	Leave English - go to my locker and then to homeroom, stop at water fountain and talk to a friend
4	08:55–09:10	Homeroom - two teachers - 17 students. Talk to two friends
5	09:10–09:15	Leave homeroom and go to the bathroom, leave and talk to 5 friends, then go to 2nd pd - French
6	09:15–10:05	2nd pd - French - go over worksheets. One teacher - 21 students
7	10:05–10:10	Leave 2nd period and walk to 3rd period - Photography w/ 2 friends.
8	10:10–10:55	3rd pd - Photography develop pictures, make prints. One teacher and 20 students
9	10:55–11:00	Leave Photography - walk to 4th period, talk to 2 friends
10	11:00–11:50	4th period - Attendance Office Assistant - run errands and call names. work w/ 2 other assistants
11	11:50–12:40	5th period - Data Processing - work w/ computers. One teacher and 18 students
12	12:40–12:45	Leave 5th period - go to my locker and leave campus for lunch with 2 friends
13	12:50– 1:35	Off campus Lunch - usually to my house
14	1:35–01:40	Return to school - go to 7th period Anatomy
15	01:40–02:30	7th period - Anatomy - listen to Oral Reports. One teacher + 30 students
16	02:30–02:50	Leave Anatomy and go to Park Dr. and see what everyone is doing. Walk w/ 3-4 friends.

Figure 3-3: Student path system through campus.

85

STIMULATING ● SEDATIVE	○ ○	STIMULATING ● SEDATIVE
INTERESTING ● BORING	○ ○	INTERESTING ● BORING
TEACHER DIRECTED ● STUDENT DIRECTED	○ ○	TEACHER DIRECTED ● STUDENT DIRECTED
FLEXIBLE ● INFLEXIBLE	○ ○	FLEXIBLE ● INFLEXIBLE
LIKE ● DISLIKE	○ ○	LIKE ● DISLIKE

Figure 3-4: Photographs of traditional and nontradtional school settings (Photos: Graham Adams, Cheryl Walker, & Henry Sanoff).

established baseline information, the activity log was found to provide the most thorough insights on the questions of who, where, and when of building use.

While descriptive information was necessary to understand what goes on in the environment, student reactions to their environment further explained their feelings. By combining photographs of existing and proposed school settings (Figure 3-4), students made comparisons and stated their preferences. The photographs represented classrooms, study areas, and circulation paths. For each question asked, there were four photographs, including one representing a setting from their school. The student responses to the questionnaire indicated a strong preference for settings that were filled with daylight, that were informal and relaxed, yet containing areas that concentrated on learning. None of the existing school settings were included in the students' choices.

The exercises identified which campus elements were most important, what portions of the existing building should be preserved, and what might constitute a suitable character. The relationships which exist in people's minds between image, decision making, and behavior are important to designers in composing the physical environment.

OBSERVING CHILDREN'S ACTIVITIES

To determine children's outdoor activities in a recently completed multifamily rental project, 150 systematic observations were made of the eight-acre planned residential environment. The site contained staggered rows of attached single-family units grouped around parking lots. Each parking lot led into a dead-end street that linked the project to a highway; pedestrian sidewalks framing the perimeter of the parking lots served each dwelling and joined the units together. Play areas with wooden benches were located at six junctures along the walkway between units. Activities which occurred were coded into categories of *work* (hanging wash, car repair, and sweeping), *general play* (exploring and camping), *biking, passive* (observing, talking, and reading), *walking, basketball, ball play* (kickball and catch), *object play* (sticks, knives, and jump ropes), *horsehoe pitching,* and *active play* (scuffling and gymnastics). Locations at which the activities were recorded included the physical elements of front stoop, backyard, public sidewalk, street, parking lots, woods, public open space, and community open space. A behavioral map of the site plan was prepared from the observations, locating activities and group size (Figure 3-5).

The distribution of activities and their cluster patterns indicated that well over one-half of the observed activity occurred in or within view of the community space, including both participants and spectators. The community space, then, functioned as a social contact center (Festinger, 1964) from which activities distributed themselves outward throughout the site, as intended in the design. The greatest behavioral density occurred where physical cues (basketball court, jungle gym, spring horse, climbing apparatus, and so forth) were perceptible and suggested prescribed behaviors to the participants. The least dense, but

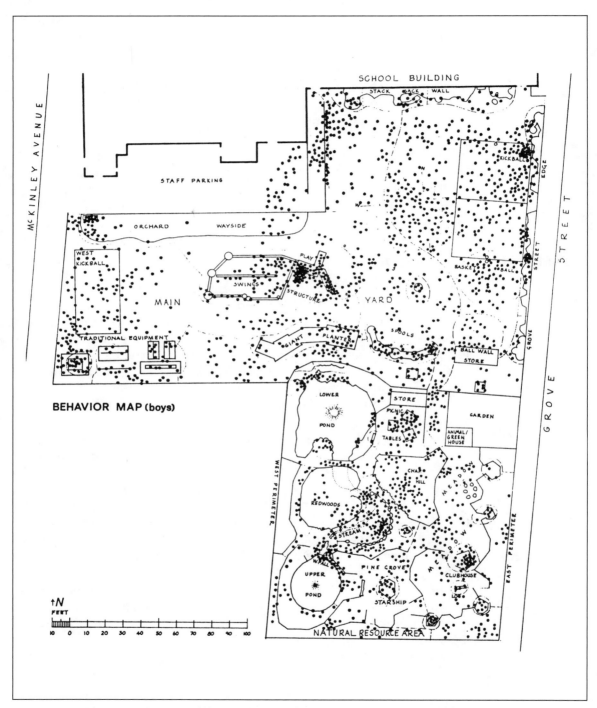

Figure 3-5: Girls' behavior map aggregated from eighteen noontime recess observation periods (Drawing: Robin Moore).

highest behavioral diversity, however, occurred in settings like back-
yards and streets which were more ambiguous, allowing participants
to interpret cues differently. Observation of the environment, then,
reinforced the known strength of the peer group in directing children
to group activities which took place in more structured settings, while
less prescribed areas allowed more individual and diverse play. The
study indicated that a variety of settings, from well-articulated to ambiguous, allows a wide range of expected and unexpected children's
behavior to occur (Sanoff & Coates, 1971).

Behavioral observation and mapping were used in researching and
designing two playgrounds in Davis, California, one a new neighborhood playground in the Village Homes solar community and the other
a redesign of the Pioneer Elementary School (Francis, 1988). One aim
of the projects was to investigate and negotiate differences between
children's and adults' design values and preferences. The behavior
mapping recorded how children were actually using the landscape,
and was useful in pointing out children's special needs, such as hiding
places, as well as demonstrating favorite places (Figure 3-6). Other

Figure 3-6: Where kids play: total observations (Drawing: Mark Francis, University
of California, Davis).

exercises included map and model making with the children, child-led tours, and interviews and meetings where both children and parents elicited each others' preferences and ideas.

Findings corroborated earlier studies which indicated children's preferences for open spaces, undefined natural areas, and claiming found places in the landscape.

MAPPING CHILDREN'S ACTIVITIES

In a UNESCO sponsored study of five nations conducted by Lynch (1977), research teams examined the way that young adolescents use their environment. Research teams in Argentina, Australia, Mexico, and Poland have looked at the way small groups of young adolescents use and value their spatial environment. The intent of this research was to suggest public policies for improving the spatial environment. The research methods relied on observation of children's behavior as well as responses to the image of their local environment.

Children were asked to draw a map of "the area you live in" (1977, p. 28). Most of the children included the location of their houses and those of their friends and bounded their maps by the places in which they were involved. Children's images of their locality revealed play patterns, friendships, and their home range. They also revealed the significance of features of their town and conceptions of their town.

The policy implications for the children in the study locales are important, particularly for social interaction and informal play. The form and regulation of local streets and small open spaces is a critical issue. Traffic hazards, underused and left-over areas, and landscaping can all be influenced by general policies.

Observing children's behavior provides additional insight into their favorite places and the way in which they use their environment. Diagrams, supplemented by photographs and notes are useful methods for recording behavior (Figure 3-7). In Melbourne, Australia, use of space outside the house lot by children is predominantly confined to the streets (Figure 3-8). Young children play in the streets because they provide the only near-to-home public space large enough for energetic games. Therefore, researcher Peter Downton (p. 109 Lynch, 1977a) began observing streetscapes. The activity in the streets was based on walking and meeting people, and as a result, rarely occurred in the same location twice. Consequently, it was necessary for the observation team to drive around looking for the action. Although there were no modifications made to the environment, various settings were being used in ways in which they were not intended, such as using steps, fences, and pavement areas for sitting.

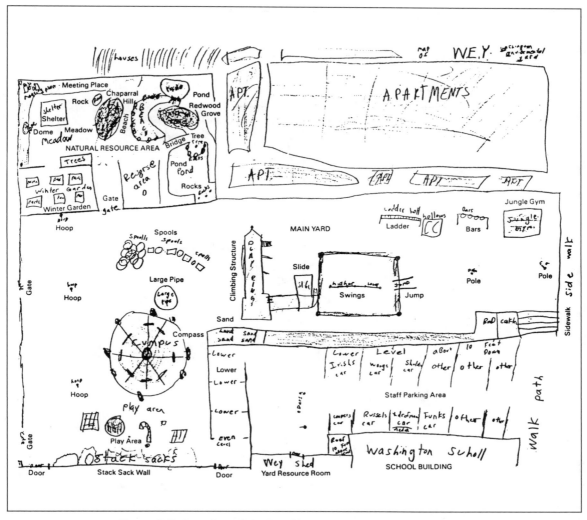

Figure 3-7: Drawing of the Yard by a nine-year-old boy. The Natural Resource Area is shown in the top right-hand corner, with many of the most significant elements noted; the Main Yard covers the middle portion of the drawing. In the bottom right-hand corner is the teachers' parking lot shown in great detail, including differences in ground level (Drawing: Robin Moore).

Since it is apparent that instantaneous records would be difficult to compile and analyze, Lynch concludes that diagrams should be accompanied by a series of still photographs as well as a videotape of some sequences of child activity. Videotapes are best suited to record activity, while diagrams and photographs describe better and more simply the place in which the activity occurs.

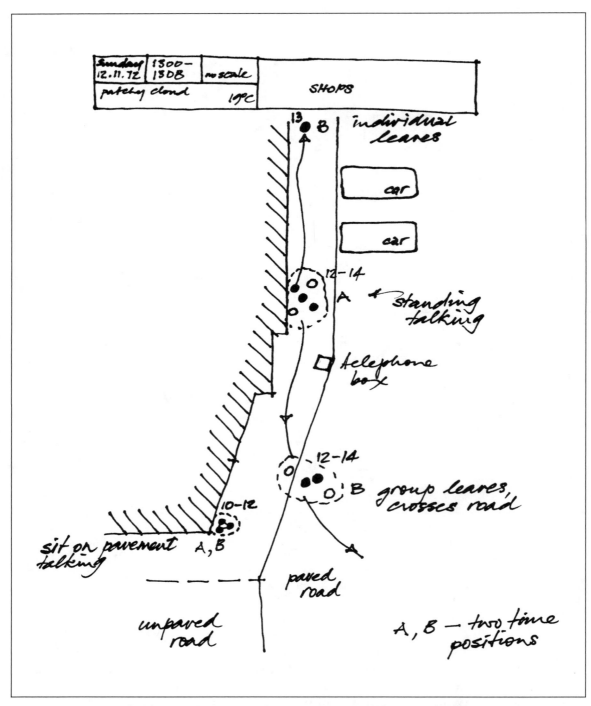

Figure 3-8: Observation of street activities, Melbourne, Australia (Drawing: Peter Downton).

TRACKING

An observation technique that concentrates on patterns of pedestrian use is described as tracking. *Tracking* is the systematic following and recording of a subject's movement. Patterns of pedestrian activity are derived from tracking a large number of subjects. Since the particular behavior of an individual is of little interest, it is unnecessary for the tracker to question or explain to the subject his or her activities. Instead, the tracker can work expeditiously to make a large number of observations that can be translated into patterns of movement.

A limited tracking study was conducted of the behavior of people who were walking around the fairgrounds during the 1962 Seattle World's Fair (Weiss & Bourteline, 1962). Observers systematically followed people, noting which events most attracted them and the sequence in which they visited the places of their choice.

The collection of data begins with the selection of a subject at a pedestrian origin point, such as a parking garage or a transit stop. Subjects should be randomly selected by using a stop watch and identifying the first person to pass a given point in a particular time interval. In a Seattle study (Grey, Winkle, Bonsteel, & Parker, 1970), data was collected about the sex and age of the subject, weather conditions, time of day and duration of track, land use at origin and destination points, and the map location of the path taken.

Since the study pertained to shopping patterns in downtown Seattle, time spent in stores was also recorded. Nearly one-third of all stops were of less than five minutes in duration, spent in purchasing a newspaper or cigarettes. The longest stops, thirty minutes or more, were recorded during the Christmas shopping season. These comprised slightly more than one-fifth of the total time spent shopping.

A pedestrian may be in the survey area for the purpose of doing one errand or of combining several. If an individual is carrying out a single mission, he or she can be identified upon entry into an area, followed (tracked), and observed until the objective is reached. On emerging from that point, the subject may again be followed until he or she leaves the survey area. Each component of the passage is a *single-transition track*. Similarly, each component of a *multi-transition track* can be regarded as a single unit, in that it has a start and a finish (Figure 3-9).

In the single-transition track, a person would be followed from a given *origin point*. The location at which the subject left the sidewalk to enter a building is termed the *destination point*. The pedestrian trip between a single origin point and a destination point is called a *transition*. In a single transition, a person is followed from one origin point to the first destination point (for example, from a drugstore to a de-

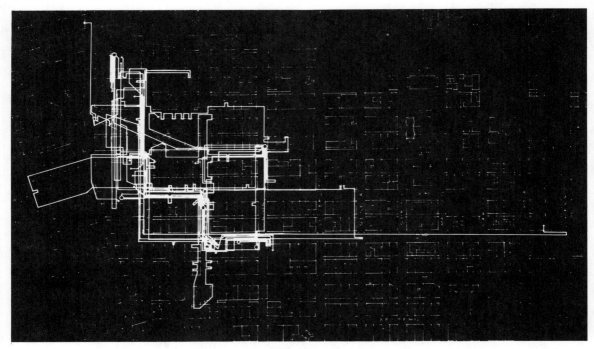

Figure 3-9: Path of multi-transition tracks, Seattle, summer 1966 (Drawing: Arthur Grey & David Bonsteel).

partment store). In a multi-transition track, a subject is tracked from an origin point to a succession of destination points.

Some origin points in the Seattle study were considered *initial* origin points, since they represented the locations where people became subjects and occurred at bus stops and parking lots. In contrast, when these points became the pedestrian's *final* destination point, they were the last place where the person was a downtown pedestrian, such as at a transit stop. A multi-transition track in the Seattle study extended from the initial origin point to the final destination of the person tracked. Thus, the track might encompass the entire pedestrian experience of a person on a downtown trip.

In addition to the geographic location of the track, the tracker recorded any intermediate stops for which the subject did not leave the sidewalk, as for window shopping or stopping at red lights. The activity of multi-transition trips can be best understood when they are observed in their entirety. Although the occurrence of identical matches may be infrequent, the accumulation of multi-transition track data is the best way to learn about long-term pedestrian behavior.

One finding of the Seattle tracking experience was that the pedestrian remained within four blocks of the point of entry regardless of how time-consuming or how varied the itinerary. From this it was concluded that, within the twenty-square-block retail area, the majority of pedestrians did their shopping within a twelve-square-block area.

DOCUMENTARY TECHNIQUES

Photography is one of the many tools available to the researcher studying behavior in the environment. Although visually observable, behavior is a small part of the complex interaction between people and their environment. Even when we have images of people in a setting, we have little sense of what they make of it or of the images themselves (Collier, 1979). The camera can provide us with insights that have been unavailable previously.

The use of photographs is a well-established practice in *ethnography*, the descriptive study of specific cultures. The social sciences, however, have been dominated by the written word. Researchers generally think of visual records as illustrative of literary issues. Even those who have studied small-scale human interactions have tended to do so from literary decriptions of the transactions. In recording the visual aspects of behavior, photography can provide much greater accuracy and much more information about complex or brief events than observation with written notes (Davis & Ayers, 1975). Photography can improve observational effectiveness by allowing the study of an event in depth of detail. The use of a camera can be particularly effective in teaching and recording individual or group behavior in a particular place, or over time.

The camera can also be used to inventory spaces, buildings, or interiors, as well as to show how people use spaces. Half a day spent with photographic equipment in a baggage sorting area revealed how the system really worked compared to what was intended and what was understood by management (Davis & Ayers, 1975). Film can be effective in tracking and recording spatial behavior over a period of time where self-reports, diaries, or observers could overlook important information. Photography can also be used to record, analyze, and communicate visual features that contribute to the image of a particular environment.

Time-lapse photography at ninety-one frames per second and five-minute film sequences were used in a study by a team of social science and landscape architecture students at the University of Massachusetts—Amherst for the redesign of a pedestrian space in a heavily used part of the campus. Pedestrian density maps were prepared for the recorded intervals; summary maps reflected major pathways and suggested needs for route clarification and greater visual accessibility (Friedman, Zimring, & Zube, 1978).

In a study conducted to understand behavior on escalators and moving sidewalks at airports, Davis and Ayers (p. 245) were interested in observing escalator approach behavior of people in groups and with young children. They were also interested in using photographic data to see if the physical characteristics of the area affected approach behavior. Photologs were used to record environmental conditions and population characteristics that would accompany the time-lapse photography. The results of the study revealed typical patterns of behavior, with people frequently checking behind them to see that their companions were following safely at an escalator approach and at the exit from a moving walkway. Two different types of approach zones were identified, the outer zone consisting of body movements in anticipation of an approach, and an inner zone that consisted mainly of minor body adjustments.

Data were gathered by three-person teams, equally dividing tasks of time-lapse movies, 35mm slides, and photolog recording. Since this study was also intended to test the phototechnology, comparisons were made between the two recording techniques, revealing that in many instances the 35mm slides were redundant.

PHOTO STREETSCAPES

The visual experience of the pedestrian users of downtown Seattle was recorded by means of a camera which could simulate the visual reality of pedestrian paths. Streetscapes, surfaces, and architectural details were recorded and analyzed by Grey, Winkle, Bonsteel, and Parker (1970), in order to understand visual patterns.

Pedestrian behavior can be seen not only as reaction to the presence of physical obstacles or to a passing vehicle, but also as a response to peripheral visual stimuli. The use of a camera to record a pedestrian's pathway experience is enhanced if the depth of focus and width of camera angle correspond to the individual's field of attention. The usefulness of the Widelux camera in providing a panoramic view equal in extent to the binocular visual field of a pedestrian is illustrated on Figure 3-10. The center photo records central vision, while those on each side record elements of peripheral vision.

Photo studies were made of principal pathways in downtown Seattle and were studied to document path sequences and to detect differences that might explain commonly expressed images of particular streets. All photos were taken at eye level in order to approximate pedestrian line of sight. The two flanking pictures in each set, which

A

B

C

Figure 3-10: Pedestrian-eye views. The visual effect of curb parking. Note feeling of confinement when cars separate pedestrians from street (Photo: Arthur Grey & David Bonsteel).

record the area of peripheral vision, suggest that perception of curb-parking acts as a barrier between the pedestrian and moving traffic. While the pedestrian may not consciously scan this peripheral area, there is an awareness of the presence of either side. Areas with no curb-parking have an equally significant impact on the experience of a particular path. The removal of automobiles from curb-parking diminishes the visual distinction between sidewalk and street.

This photographic approach is a step toward a more objective analysis of perceived experience and characteristics of sequential pathways. While photos can record field conditions, they do not represent the actual experience.

TRANSFORMING STREET SCENES

Photographic simulations have been widely used to determine user's preferences. In a streetscape study aimed at specifying the physical elements that influence judgments, researchers Winkel, Malek, and Thiel (1970) selected a segment of a street in Seattle for their investigation. Since the study team was concerned about every combination of relevant physical variable while maintaining a constant pattern for the nonphysical variables, modifications of visual scenes were made by retouching photographs of the environments they represented. Black and white photographs (Figure 3-11) were used in conjunction with an extensive list of polar opposite adjectives. Ten photographs were taken of each route "as it is." Transformations were made by eliminating objects from the street environment such as billboards or utility poles, and an additional set of ten slides was produced.

Observers were seated in front of a screen and viewed the "as it is" sequence. After the viewing, the observers were asked to rate the sequence using the verbal scale. After completing this task, the observers were then asked to view the transformed slide sequence and comment on whether or not changes were detected. The elimination sequence, as shown on Figures 1 to 4, were most noticed when utility poles and overhead wires were removed. Some of the respondents, however, were surprised at the dull and uninteresting quality of the resulting environment.

PHOTOGRAPHICALLY STUDYING BEHAVIOR

The locations of open space use were photographically observed to assess their connections to pedestrian flow patterns and their actual use (Grey, Winkel, Bonsteel, & Parker, 1970). In Seattle's Westlake Mall, a pictorial record was kept on people's use, their length and

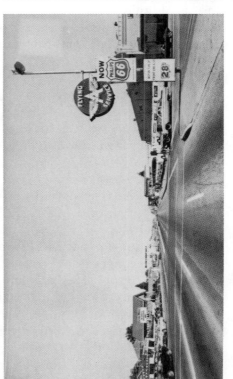

Figure 3-11: A Seattle street scene: (a) No modifications. (b) Route minus utility poles and overhead wires. (c) Route minus utility poles, overhead wires, and billboards. (d) Route minus utility poles, overhead wires, billboards, and other signs (Photos: Gary Winkel, Roger Malek, Philip Thiel).

99

purpose of visit, and the type of user. The open spaces were also assessed on their ability to attract, hold, or channel pedestrians in at one end and out at the other.

Behavior patterns were photographically recorded at various intervals throughout the day, and during different kinds of weather conditions. The photographic pattern was intentionally randomized, though particular staged events were recorded.

The camera was in full view of pedestrians, but an effort was made to give the impression that it was not in operation when the subjects were looking in that direction. The photographer used a long cable release and looked in another direction when recording events in order to avoid camera shyness. The study was conducted over a period of fifteen months, during which 1800 photographs were compiled to provide an overall picture of space use, space characteristics, and pedestrian flow patterns.

The open spaces were divided into those that were occupiable by people and described as *habitable* and *visual,* and those where buildings and leftovers in the street pattern created wasted space. The factors that were considered to influence space use were specific locations in the shopping sequence that were used to view a natural scene, a memorial, a building, or a special event. Researchers found that proximity to pedestrian activity areas was extremely important, since planned spaces that were off the beaten track were virtually unused, regardless of their habitability.

The pedestrian mall was the subject of further analysis to determine the use of benches located on the street edge of the sidewalks, and the effects of staged events and weather conditions on their use. Five station points were set up for making photographs of the six benches (Figure 3-12). The stations were close enough to record facial expressions, body attitudes, and interpersonal reactions under varying conditions of sun and shade. Ages of the bench users were estimated to the nearest ten-year period and included categories such as retired, shopper, tourist, and others. Stations were in operation from 10:30 A.M. to 3:30 P.M. on a clear day in August. All benches were photographed at quarter-hour intervals, and the procedure was repeated at intervals over a period of several months.

The photographs revealed that the shoppers and others used the benches mainly during the noon hour. The retired came for long periods throughout the day. A majority of the users were males over fifty years of age. Benches isolated between moving currents of people had shorter periods of occupancy. Two general types of people used the mall: retired and others. Others consisted of tourists and shoppers

Figure 3-12: The bench users in the mall and the central business district in Seattle (Photo: Arthur Grey & David Bonsteel).

who used the mall for a single activity, such as an event, or in a sequence of activities.

The results of this photographic study were of considerable interest because it had not been realized that two populations patronized the mall and that their needs were not the same. The study showed that the retired were the important users of the mall and of open spaces in the central business district as well.

STEREOSCOPIC PHOTOGRAPHY

A primary school in New South Wales, Australia, was the location for a study which monitored activities within an open-plan area of the school that was used to enter three adjacent classrooms. The aim of this project was to record photographically the extent of use and the range of activity settings at random times during a week of normal school activities.

Activities were recorded stereoscopically by two Nikon cameras that were time-synchronized to record at random intervals during a six-hour period (Figure 3-13). The choice of stereoscopic photography was based on the belief that the full meaning of real space is lost in conventional photographic recording because the images of people and furniture are all brought into a single plane. The addition of a second slide or print, taken as part of a stereopair, can provide additional information about the grouping of people and their position in space. In a primary school, where children's activities are constantly changing, and groups are continuously being restructured, stereoscopic studies can supplement graphic plottings of those activities. In addition, photographic results can also supplement the results of studies which require the presence of trained observers.

The open-plan area served thirty children and three teachers. Each of the three adjacent classrooms had a folding wall along the open area, as well as a folding wall between the other classrooms. The teachers, then, had the option of combining classrooms, including part of the open-plan space with their classroom, or moving out into the larger space.

With the time-lapse photographic method, various sizes of groups, ranging from one to sixty children, were recorded for less than half of the recorded time interval. The majority of the activities recorded children in small groups, while the entire class was observed twenty-five percent of the recorded time. The sequence of activities shown for a typical day began with taking apart the small group table. The table was then brought back to the hexagonal form when four adults arrived with items pupils could purchase; then purchasing. A small group of

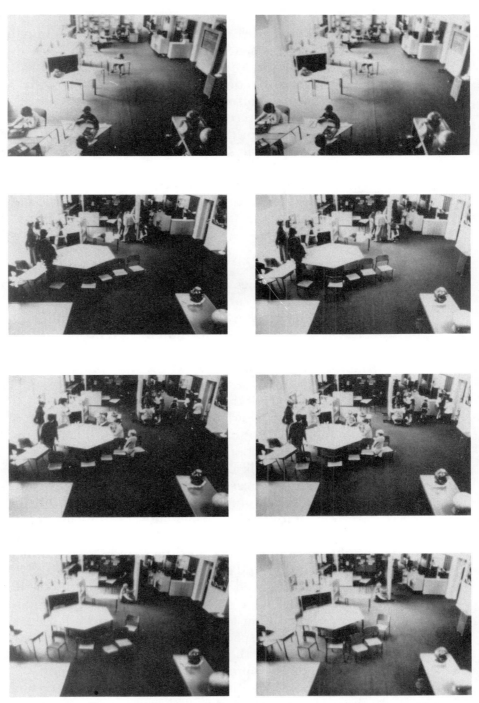

Figure 3-13: Photo time-sampling in an open-plan classroom in New South Wales, Australia.

children were also observed, in both stereopairs, at a mobile chalk-board. This activity continued for two children into the lunch period.

The arrangement of furniture in the open-plan area changed very little during the week. One classroom extended its territory into the open-plan area in order to create a transitional zone. Major rearrangements occurred infrequently.

Following the recording of space use, the three teachers were shown the stereopairs for their comments. The occupancy recording method using stereoscopic sampling enabled the teachers to see and understand the actual space use. The infrequent use of the open-plan area, which constituted eighty percent of the total classroom space, was reinterpreted by the users themselves. The objective measurement of actual space use was subsequently understood at a practical level.

SONIC MAPPING

While most studies in perception address visual information, there is also an auditory component of the environment which can be identified and mapped graphically. The character of the soundscape may be less apparent to sensorally-unimpaired people who interpret their surroundings through a mixture of sensory cues, but the critical importance of auditory experiences for blind, and the psychological impoverishment felt by deaf individuals indicate the effect and potential of this part of the physical world.

To expand knowledge of the urban soundscape, field studies were conducted in Boston (Southworth, 1969) comparing fifteen subjects' reported perceptions of sounds and sights during a two- and three-quarter-mile walk through the center of the city. The study investigated changes over time and under various weather conditions, the uniqueness and singularity of local sounds in different city settings, the extent to which activities and spatial forms were communicated by sounds, and the reported delightfulness of sounds in various locations. Subjects were grouped in threes, and described their perceptions on tape recorders and maps, characterizing most- and least-liked settings. Each trio consisted of auditory subjects who were blindfolded; visual subjects who wore ear plugs and muffs; and visual-auditory subjects with normal sight and hearing. The trip followed a course from the historic, tightly-spaced Beacon Hill residential area to India Wharf, passing through the government center, the Haymarket, the financial district, the shopping area, and Boston Common.

The most identifiable sound districts contained visible exterior activity and had unique spatial characteristics such as tight, narrow, hard street spaces; confined alleyways and tunnels; or the open waterfront and Common. "Responsive spaces," where subjects could hear echoes of their own sounds, were more clearly perceived and felt to be more meaningful. Settings had more clarity in the early morning, evening, or on weekends, when traffic sounds were less likely to homogenize and mask sounds. Snow and rain shrank the sonic spaciousness of the city and made it quieter.

The paths along the thirty-three points of the trip had different sight and sound values for the various subjects (Figure 3-14). Not surprisingly, auditory subjects reported more sounds than visual-auditory subjects. The visual subjects perceived the city as sad, lonely, and two-dimensional; robbed of what Southworth called "the healing salve of sound," they found more imperfections in the environment. While the auditory participants commented on the peacefulness of the waterfront, the calls of the gulls, and the feel of the wind, their sight-ed counterparts saw the same as ugly, dull, smelly, and dirty. Visual-auditory subjects recalled combinations of sights and sounds which made areas memorable, such as an airplane taking off some distance from the shore. Similarly, the shopping area was seen only as gaudy and vulgar; heard as lively and exciting; and seen and heard as satis-fying, jazzy, and interesting. Preferred sonic settings were unique and informative as well as responsive; least-preferred settings were unin-formative, redundant, and stressful, having sounds of high frequency and intensity. Preferred sonic-visual settings were those of contrast and animation, with sound- and sight-related events.

Results of the studies not only reinforce the established importance of the auditory component of the existing environment, but suggest the potential of *sonic design* in enhancing environment. Adding sonic characters can mask noise, ameliorate visually unpleasant or uninter-esting areas, increase the identity of settings, and provide novel and pleasant experiences. *Sonic signs* identifying local activities, conveying public information, and calling out landmarks could be better used to give special character and added dimension to urban scenes.

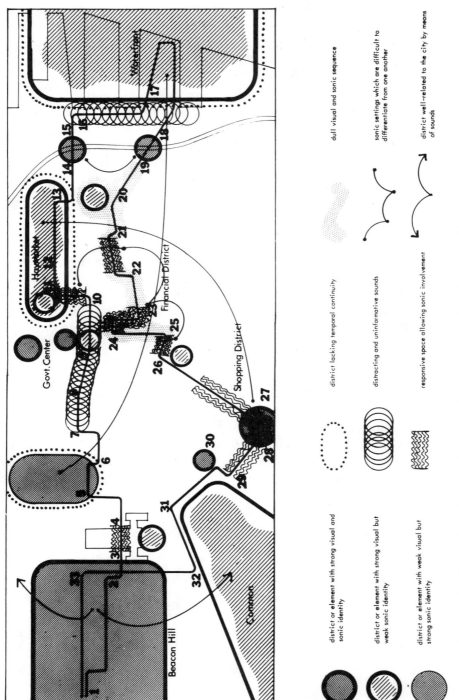

Figure 3-14: Evaluation of part of the Boston Soundscape (Michael Southworth).

4

VISUAL NOTATION

Systems of observation and notation have been developed with a view to standardizing the reporting of behavioral events. Anthropologist Hall (1963) developed a notation system or proxemic behavior when it became apparent that people from different cultures interacting with each other would attach different meanings to the same distance between them. "What was close to an American might be distant to an Arab" (Hall, p. 1003). Visual anthropology expands the recording capability of notation systems by providing photographic evidence with accuracy, which extends the credibility and scope of descriptive records (Collier, 1986).

For environmental designers, spatial definition, or the perception of the degree of openness or enclosure of a given occupied space is the common concern (Thiel, Harrison, & Alden, 1986). The perception of our visual world, however, is a dynamic process. Spaces, surfaces, events and their meanings cannot be experienced simultaneously, but must be experienced in some sequence of time (Thiel, 1961). Systematic methods of recording the dynamic organization of space in buildings and in cities is the principal reason for the development of notation systems.

Kevin Lynch's *Image of the City,* written in 1960, is one of the key works on environmental perception. Lynch's notation system for describing the city has had a significant influence on researchers, designers, and planners in many parts of the world. His primary focus was the visual quality of cities and finding ways to delight in the urban landscape. He was concerned with the legibility of the cityscape, or the ease with which the parts, such as districts, landmarks, nodes, and pathways, can be organized into a coherent pattern. Although legibility is not the only property of a beautiful city, it is important for the design of large-scale complex urban environments. To understand this, Lynch argues, is not only to consider the physical properties of the city, but how the city is perceived by its inhabitants. Structuring and identifying the environment is a function of its imageability, or the mental pictures carried by city inhabitants. It is the unique combination of shape, colors, or arrangements that enables the making of identifiable mental images of the environment.

The building blocks for making differentiated environments are paths, edges, landmarks, nodes, and regions. Paths constitute the line of motion, which should have clarity of direction. Objects along the path can help to sharpen the effect of that motion. Events along the path, such as landmarks which are in contrast with its context, also facilitate clarity of image. Edges provide the opportunity to differentiate and evoke the sensations of being inside or outside. Nodes are the anchor points in cities; this type of element implies a distinct place, one that is defined with clear boundaries and an intensity of use. A sense of the whole is achieved when these elements are integrated into a sequentially perceived experience, where parts are perceived only in context.

To understand fully the role of environmental images, and to learn what forms make strong images, Lynch conducted two studies to compare the idea of imageability with the visual reality. His technique of image analysis consisted of a field reconnaissance of the area made by a trained observer, who mapped the presence of various elements, their visibility, and their perceived strength. These subjective judgments were based on the visual appearance of these elements in the field.

Residents were also interviewed to determine the characteristics of their images of the city. They were asked to sketch a map of the city, describe a series of trips through the city, and list its most distinctive parts. Lynch then discussed city image in terms of paths, edges, districts, nodes, and landmarks, through a series of maps which were constructed of the three cities he investigated—Los Angeles, Boston, and Jersey City.

The independent field analysis accurately predicted the group image derived from the interviews, though neglected minor elements important for automobile circulation. The sketch map, as a projective test, allows for a maximum of structuring by the individual; in the case of the three cities, composite sketch maps correlate well with the composite of verbal interviews.

ENCODING

To understand the sequential experience of architectural and urban spaces, Thiel (1961) developed a sequence-experience notation system. The work was stimulated by the discontinuous nature of sketches and photographs, and the fact that the viewpoint of those projects was remote from the actual experience. Thiel, therefore, proposed a graphic notation system for recording the continuity of space sequence experiences. Based on the concept of visual cues, which are environmental qualities that suggest three-dimensionality, Thiel proposed that all cues exist in terms of the visual qualities and quantities of *surfaces* (two-dimensional plane forms), *screens* (perforated screens or closely spaced objects), and *objects* (three-dimensional convex forms existing as visual entities). The experience of space results from the visual perception of light-defined relationships between positions and qualities of surfaces, screens, and objects. The attributes of these space-establishing elements are: position, size, direction, number, shape, color, and texture. Surfaces, screens, and objects categorized in three basic positions; over, side, and under define form (Figure 4-1).

Additional classifications related to vagueness or explicitness in defining a space. In this continuum, space-defining elements that are random or ambiguous were termed *vagues*. The more explicitly defined spaces that result from complete and contiguous surfaces were called *volumes*. An intermediate position on the scale, where forms result from the variety of positions between surfaces, screens, and objects, were called *spaces*. If a space or volume had any one overall dimension at least two times greater than any other dimension, it was called a *run*. The remaining spaces and volumes were termed *areas*. Thus, a given spatial sequence might be described as a vague, a space run, a space area, a volume run, or a volume area.

Since architectural and urban spaces are visually connected, a further classification into *merges, ports,* and *ends* defined the point of juncture where one space flows into the other. Factors conditioning the experience of a space include the path chosen, the direction, and the rate of travel. Spatial sequences can then be graphed with dimensions, duration lines, and directions of vertical movements. The space score has certain analogies with a musical score, and borrows terms from musical notation.

Thiel's classification system recognizes the simultaneity of spatial experience and attempts to codify the space-defining elements. As an example, driving in a car (a volume) also offers the experience of a

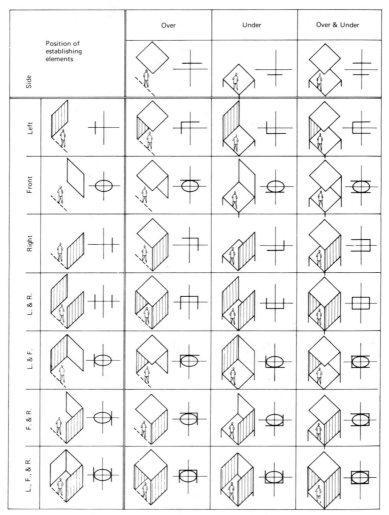

Figure 4-1: Space-form notation for orthogonal surfaces (Reprinted by permission of Philip Thiel).

street (a secondary space) and a town located in a mountain valley (tertiary space).

Although Thiel recognized that spatial meaning is conveyed through signs and symbols, he suggested that they may be included in this system in the form of written annotations. With increased use and familiarity, such meanings may also become codified. For example, he proposed graphic symbols for Kevin Lynch's five circulation elements of the city: paths, edges, districts, nodes, and landmarks.

Recognizing that the objective of environmental designers is to "create local scenes of distinctive character," Thiel, Harrison, and Alden (1986) conducted studies to establish the relative importance of his SEEs (Space Establishing Elements) in the perception of the enclosing effect of architectural surfaces (Figure 4-2). Thiel hypothesized that

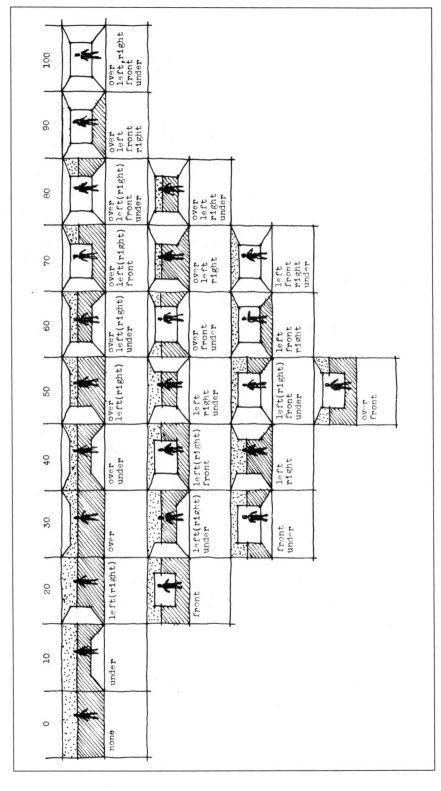

Figure 4-2: Scale of explicitness (Reprinted by permission of Philip Thiel).

111

the enclosing effect is a function of the position of surfaces, and that their relative importance could be weighted in the ratio of 1:2:3 for horizontal under, vertical side and horizontal over positions, respectively (Thiel, Harrison, & Alden, 1986).

In the first experiment, thirty-five college students were presented with a set of twenty-four black-and-white line drawings on 8½- by 11-inch cards, each depicting the same architectural interior space drawn in one-point perspective, furnished with the same table and six chairs and standing female scale figure. Each drawing showed a different combination of intact, complete enclosing surfaces, textured with equally spaced straight and parallel lines, ranging from "least explicit" with furniture and figure only, to "most explicit" with five enclosing surfaces and the objects (Figure 4-3). The students were asked to order the twenty-two remaining drawings between the established poles of "openness" and "closedness."

In the second part, the students were given a drawing of the complete enclosure condition, and were asked to number the parts of the

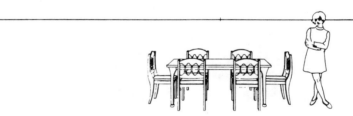

Figure 4-3: (a) "Least explicit" and (b) "most explicit" spaces (Reprinted by permission of Philip Thiel).

structure from 1 (most enclosing) to n (least enclosing) allowing for attributions of parts of equal rank if appropriate.

The results of the experiments confirmed Thiel's hypothesis. The overhead surface was judged to be the most enclosing, the underneath least, and the sides of intermediate value, in the ratio predicted. The studies suggest potential for designers in determining the perception of spaces of different scales, proportions, and shapes, and of different combinations of surfaces, screens, objects, and other elements identified in the notation system.

MOTATION

Motation is a notation system devised by Halprin (1965) to conceptualize the design of movement. Notation in movement has its basis in dance; *labanotation* records dances for comparison, analysis, and reconstruction, using a detailed system for recording the precise movements of arms, legs, step patterns, and attitudes. Motation derives from the changing qualities of the environment, with variations in the speed that we move through and around the environment. Motation is also related to the techniques of film animation, where individual pictures are related in time to form apparent movement (1965, p. 128).

The Motation system uses a standardized form, called a *frame*, that can be joined end to end to form a movement composition. Frames, read vertically from bottom to top, are notated with a series of symbols that constitute the alphabet, which produces the Motation language (Figure 4-4). Symbols represent forms in the landscape such as hills, mountains, and buildings, as well as cars and people. A Horizontal Track, composed of a row of large frames, is used to map the path of travel, while a Vertical Track, a stack of smaller frames, records what is seen in the path ahead. Speed and distance are recorded on either side of the Vertical Track; irregular spacing of symbols indicates a change in speed. The Horizontal and Vertical Tracks are read together to characterize the three-dimensional quality of the environment. The combined tracks, which describe horizontal and vertical space, time, and distance, can be read to plot the movement patterns of a person at various speeds.

Motation, argues Halprin, is not a substitute for traditional visual plans and elevations. Rather, it produces abstract representations of three-dimensional visual experience. As with any new language, time and effort is required before competence in its use is acquired. The system is perceived as a tool for recording existing, or designing new, conditions involving movement. It is capable of recording the character of movement through space at pedestrian scales as well as motion at the speed of freeways.

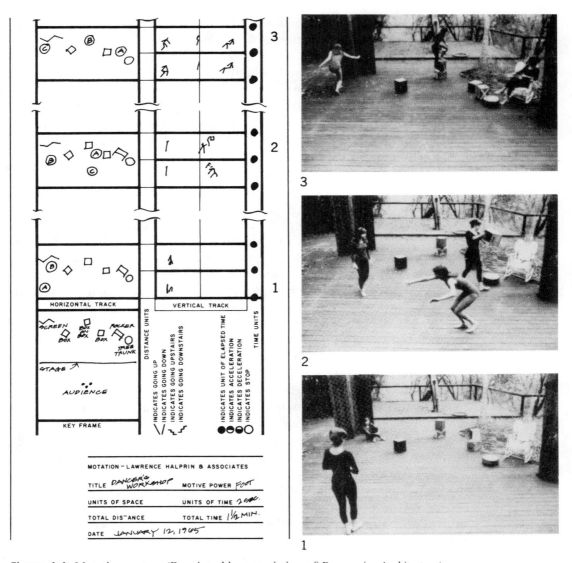

Figure 4-4: Motation system (Reprinted by permission of *Progressive Architecture*).

RECORDING HIGHWAY SEQUENCES

Consideration of the aesthetics of highways grew out of Donald Apple-yard's (Appleyard, Lynch & Meyer, 1964) concern with the visual formlessness of cities and the prospect of designing visual sequences for the observer in motion. Arguing that the highway landscape was a neglected opportunity in the design of cities, Appleyard proposed that the view from the road could be a dramatic play of space and motion and of light and texture. Any attempt at changing this view from the road would require recording, analyzing, and communicating its visual sequences.

Many of the elements that comprise a visual sequence can be recorded in conventional ways by detailed topographic and land use maps. Aerial and ground views capturing the visual sequence can be further enhanced by perspective sketches. Generally, this type of information presents a static view of the sequence and typically presents an undifferentiated mass of information requiring the user to reconstruct the third dimension. While motion pictures are useful in conveying a sense of motion, there were many cost and technical obstacles that motivated the development of a simple graphic technique for recording visual sequences. Such a technique would allow the rapid communication and comparison of sequence alternatives (p. 21).

The abstract notation of motion and space developed by Appleyard borrowed heavily from the previous work of Lynch (1960) and Thiel (1961). The recording of such roadside details as changes in lights, signs, rails, and paving texture was easy. The apparent meaning of the landscape was analyzed in terms of locational orientation and the experience of motion.

Perception of motion and space includes self-motion, such as speed and direction, and the motion of the visual field: passing alongside, overhead, or underneath. Spatial characteristics include the position of enclosing surfaces, proportions of space enclosed, quality of light, and the views which direct the eye to different aspects of the enclosed space.

Another dimension of a highway run is sense of orientation, referring to the mental image of highway setting, which in turn relies on what is perceived as well as memories of past experiences. Elements that constitute highway image include paths, nodes, districts, edges, and landmarks. Paths refer to the observer's movement lines (highways, walkways); edges are lines which appear as boundaries; nodes are focal points such as intersections; and landmarks are reference points. Districts are those areas that are easily identifiable.

An orientation sequence diagram would describe the continuity of the path, the elements associated with the path, and the location of decision points. The principal goals of the trip would also be identified, showing when they become visible. Finally, the location, strength, and relation of imageable elements outside the environment would be noted. A shorthand system was developed to identify constituent elements, shown along a vertical axis (Figure 4-5). The space and motion diagram is located on the same axis to the same scale of elapsed time as the orientation diagram.

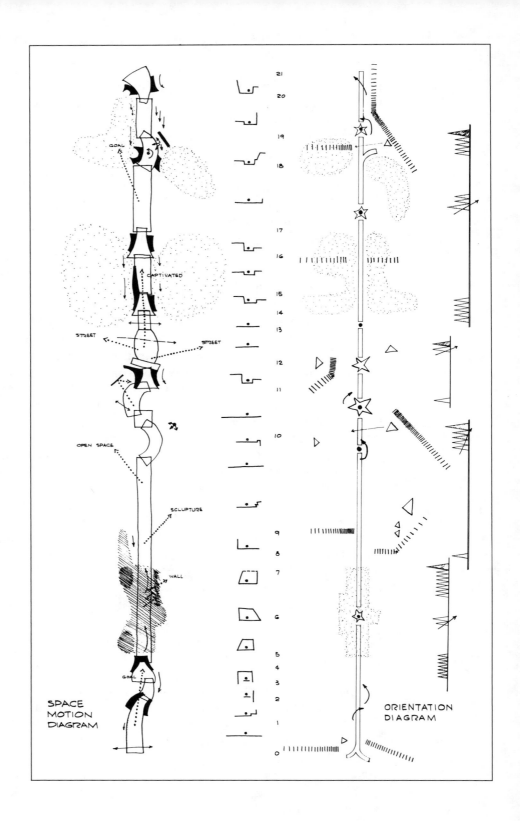

SPACE
MOTION
DIAGRAM

ORIENTATION
DIAGRAM

TOWNSCAPE

The word *townscape* signifies something more than the complex of built and unbuilt spaces that comprise the urban landscape. Townscape is the product of many shaping influences. Although climate and topography may influence urban layout, there are numerous economic and political decisions which are translated into spatial development and into the appearance of buildings we inhabit. The townscape often mirrors the life-style of the people who create it, or who use it. Townscape is the visual panorama of the way we put together our architectural surroundings.

To experience townscape is to experience visual and sensuous insight into our surroundings, the visual world of scapes. Cullen's (1971) definition of townscape is both simple and useful: "One building is architecture, but two buildings is townscape. For as soon as two buildings are juxtaposed, the art of townscape is released." Unfortunately, the appreciation of townscape is not a natural outcome of living in cities; often it has to be acquired. Certainly it can be argued that, based on the visual blight we endure, either few people possess an aesthetic appreciation of their surroundings, or if they are sensitive in this way, they have no means of altering the condition of their environment.

One strategy for getting in touch with the environment is described by Goodey (1977) as "the sensory walk." Experiencing townscape through a sensory walk serves as a foundation for descriptive, analytical, or experimental activity. The sensory walk is an opportunity to become acquainted with the familiar and to re-examine the world through senses and emotions. The organization of linked activities begins with being open to what the environment offers. Freeing the senses can be encouraged by removing one sense so that more reliance is placed on another. For example, a blindfolded person experiencing the environment may absorb sounds, smells, and textures differently than a sighted person. The sensory walk is initially unstructured and entails looking at surfaces, edges, textures, and colors. Steering cards (Figure 4-6) provide an element of structure to exploration. A set of symbols provides a guidance system for the walk, based on selecting symbol cards as cues. Sensing cards include see, hear, smell, touch, and taste. Movement cards suggest direction and speed. Additional cards Ask, Tell, Draw, and Write. Ask and Tell imply communication with people en route, the gathering of experiences, and the passing of information.

Town scores are a more structured format for experiencing the environment. The concept of a "score," like a musical score, structures users' activities, but allows room for improvisation (Halprin, 1969).

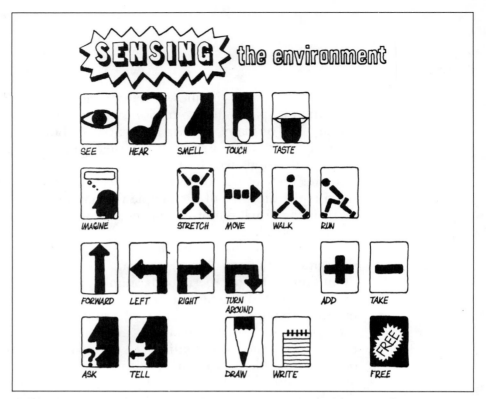

Figure 4-6: Graphic symbols used as a guidance system for a sensory walk (Drawing by Brian Goodey and Walter Menzies).

Goodey (1977) constructed a town score for Abingdon, Oxon, (in the U.K.) requiring participants to carry out specific activities at a number of identified locations along the route. With the aid of a map, participants were instructed to take various roads and discuss immediate impressions of the place. Next they were to search for a place to sit and absorb the smells, sounds, and other sensations of the area. The following sequences included walking back to the town center, finding a place to eat to discuss impressions with a resident, and finally proceeding back to the starting point and identifying the most salient features of the route.

Townscape notation provides a method for recording visual experiences. The purpose of its use is to engage participants in looking at the everyday environment; "to get a feeling for it"; and to evaluate the impact of the environment emotionally and aesthetically. The formulation of the notation is based on the assessment of opposites occurring within the townscape, and giving it an identifiable visual composition. The observer, standing at one viewing point, is asked to see a group of buildings which appear from that position to be *orderly* or *disorderly; vertical* or *horizontal* (Figure 4-7). Townscape notation identifies

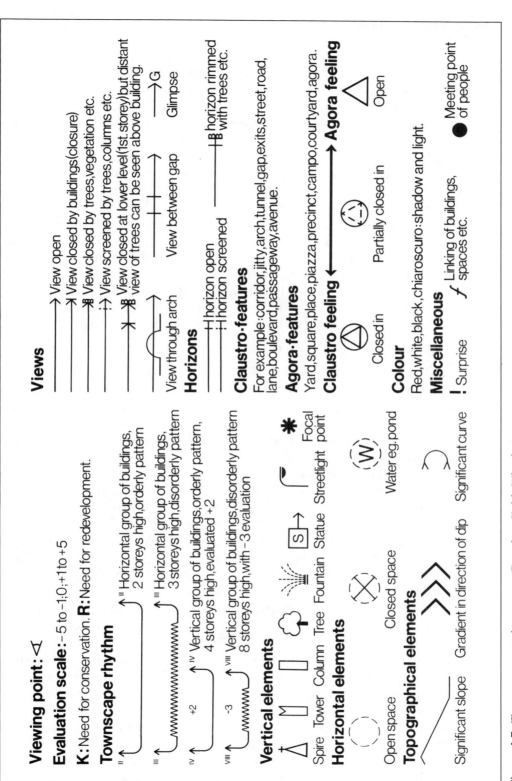

Figure 4-7: Townscape notation system (Drawing: Keith Wheeler).

119

claustro-features, such as a small courtyard; or *agora-features,* which give a feeling of openness. Similarly, there are near views and distant views; wide open views, such as horizons; and closed views, such as glimpses. Since people respond differently to groupings of buildings or streetscapes, an evaluation scale is used to record positive and negative values.

The notation system can be used by groups, who should familiarize themselves with the notation symbols before selecting a route to travel. The route should be chosen to move towards a focal point, with three intermediate viewing points at which observations can be noted. Progressing toward a focal point enables observers to experience *serial vision.* Viewing points encompass a field of vision of 180 degrees, and each requires a separate set of notations. Base maps must be provided for marking routes and viewing points (Figure 4-8). In concluding discussions, comments about the visual quality of the townscape as well as illustrations of how the route could be improved should be shared.

AWARENESS WALKS

Awareness walks and trails attempt to add significance to a particular place, and to encourage the observer to get the most from a given area. The walk typically provides historical background and may be associated with an illustrated guide. In the features observed, a walk may indicate planning problems or social issues, as well as offer aesthetic appreciation and enjoyment of what has been preserved. A trail often challenges the visitor to explore, demands a questioning approach, and invites the user to appraise the quality of what is observed and experienced.

Historic architecture has been the major focus of much guided touring, and specialist groups have provided the opportunities for guided walks through significant buildings and sites. The protection of buildings of historic interest and the conservation of the special character of neighborhoods and towns has stimulated considerable interest in the development of walks and trails. More recently, walks and trails have been developed in the belief that residents as well as visitors should be aware of the aesthetic assets of a particular place. Assisting the community in discovering itself has provided considerable incentive for walk and trail development. As a tool for understanding of and exploration in the environment, the walk or trail manages perception of the environment and directs the senses to specific sites and sights which constitute a precoded conceptual map.

Halprin has used awareness walks with community groups as an introduction to the planning process, inviting participants to take part

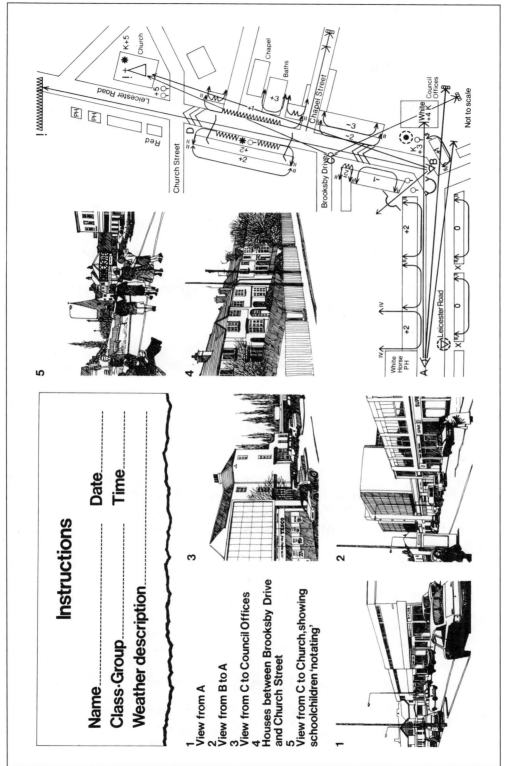

Figure 4-8: Townscape notation of a part of Oadby, England, shopping center (Drawing: Keith Wheeler).

121

in a downtown walk with specific stopping points. A walking route can also be related to longer journeys by car or by public transport. Although the range of purposes for a walk are limitless, it is necessary to stress that those producing walks or trails should have a clear idea about purpose, which can be enjoyment, education, or stimulating an interest in the planning or improvement of an area. Winders and Gray (1973) advocated that the aim of trails be to:

- arouse interest in the townscape and in the ways in which it has evolved;
- discover the processes which are currently shaping the urban environment;
- encourage a critical evaluation of the visual quality of the urban scene;
- develop the skills necessary for an analysis of the urban environment.

Factors to consider in the development and assessment of an awareness walk are route safety, accessibility for the handicapped, parking accessibility, clarity of instructions, user convenience, and possible invasion of privacy.

TRANSLATION

This exploratory study (Sanoff, 1970b) proposed to establish clues about the relationship between the socially perceived neighborhood and its physical boundaries, in order to describe their degree of correspondence. The friendship patterns established here are clearly a measure of actual behavior, and should be interpreted in the context of attitudes which appear to be relatively consistent within the population group.

A survey was conducted in the southeast section of Raleigh, North Carolina, based on 100 interviews of a randomly selected sample of households. Information of various kinds was collected about activity patterns in order to arrive at a dynamic description of a "subjective" neighborhood. Here, the use of multiple criteria for boundary definition was explored. Spatial patterns were directly represented by plotting them on a map. In addition to indicating perceived boundaries, each respondent was asked to indicate locations of the following:

The neighborhood center   Place of work
Three best friends   Major neighborhood organizations
Closest relatives   Previous residence
Primary shopping place

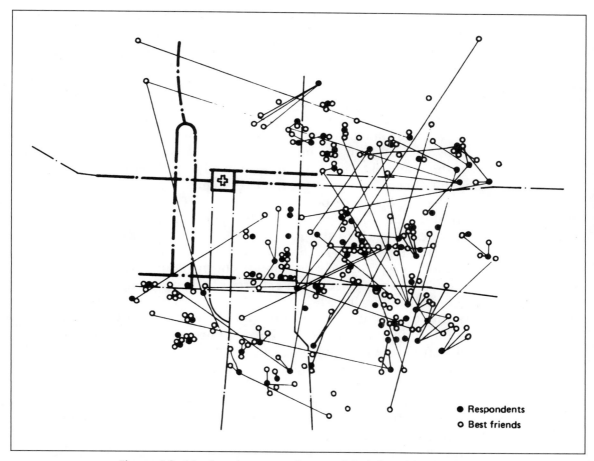

Figure 4-9: Map locating respondents and their best friends in a Raleigh, North Carolina, neighborhood (Drawing: Henry Sanoff).

all in reference to his or her own current residence. It was then possible to draw links from the home to each of the above and to aggregate the resulting collections of links (Figure 4-9).

In low-income communities where people tend to be housebound, it was hypothesized that neighboring behavior is closely related to the residents' verbal specification of their friendship patterns. It was also assumed that the image of the neighborhood and its physical boundaries are strongly influenced by the locality in which social interaction occurs. This implies that institutions generally associated with the neighborhood (that is, center, school, shopping) may not coincide with or be included in the residents' image of their neighborhood. The study area was a black section of the city where there is considerable relocation, with a relatively small amount of in-migration from the rural areas.

The location of the respondents' best friends was diagrammed and linked to their residential location. The emerging friendship patterns indicated that the highest percentage of best friends, and the highest frequency of personal contact, occurred on the respondent's own street. The findings corresponded with Young and Wilmott's studies (1957), indicating that working class families in England tend to draw their friends from the immediate locale. Friendship patterns outside of the immediate area that are sustained over several years are often a result of contact made in former residential locations.

The surveyed respondents were asked to draw the boundaries around their neighborhood, as they perceived it, on a map of the city of Raleigh. Each of the 100 individual maps was then superimposed on a master map. The neighborhood descriptions drawn by the respondents were clearly descriptions of the boundaries of their friendship patterns, since their church and shopping locations were generally not included within the boundaries of their perceived neighborhood. Though the neighborhoods were obvious, they were also highly individualistic. Major thoroughfares emanating from the center did divide the city into physical as well as perceptual sectors. Physical barriers, such as a waterway, an arterial road, and a railroad track, also imposed a danger or a threat.

Respondents used the name of the street on which they lived as the name of their neighborhood. The concept of a neighborhood center appeared ambiguous to many of the residents: to some, it implied their own house, to others, it implied important landmarks in the city—generally outside of their own subjective neighborhood—while most could not identify a center.

The church was the central source for organized activities. Church-goers traveled to outlying rural areas as well as throughout the city to participate in services and attend functions. The church was the major institution outside the home where social contacts were made and developed. Participation in these social activities frequently outweighed considerations of locational accessibility.

Southeast Raleigh is frequently spoken of as a discrete area, since people residing in other areas of the city refer to it as if it were a single entity. Yet it was clear that the area was bounded differently for different people. For most of the residents of the survey area, their territory was a very small part of southeast Raleigh. Often the public image and descriptions of various neighborhoods in this area did not correspond with the residents' descriptions. Similar studies in Boston's West End (Fried & Gleicher, 1961) indicated that the greater one's personal commitments in the area, in the form of close contact, the greater the likelihood of highly positive feelings about the area as a whole.

Neighboring relationships were of particular importance, both in their own right and in their effect on more general feelings about the area. In the West End of Boston, as well as in southeast Raleigh, kin are often neighbors. There are many interrelated friendship networks. Mutual help in household activities, too, was both possible and frequent. These characteristics are similar to those of many folk communities, where there is considerable overlap in the types of existing relationships.

RSVP CYCLES

In his work in community design, Lawrence Halprin articulated and applied a motation-like system for coordinating group creativity. *The RSVP Cycles: Creative Processes in the Human Environment* (1969) set forth the cyclical process of discovering and implementing objectives. The four ingredients in the RSVP process are *resources, the score, valuaction,* and *performance.* The first category includes all of the knowable and controllable quantities in a given situation—the human and physical resources, motivations, and aims, or what Halprin described as "what you have to work with." The score, similar to a score in dance or music, is the vehicle for participation, a set of instructions directing someone to carry out an activity, which can communicate process to other people in other places and times. Valuaction (a combination of evaluation, feedback, and decision, with an emphasis on action) is the critical response of the participants, in which discussion takes place, alternatives are reviewed, and selections are made, all in an atmosphere that encourages comments and criticisms. In the performance, objectives of the participants are realized, in a previously determined manner. It is the synthesis of the four parts that Halprin believes makes the process effective.

The RSVP cycles form the core of Halprin's "Take Part Process," of design. Community workshops begin with the development of a common language of shared experiences. Objectives, rather than goals, are identified, to encourage more dynamic alternatives and allow more direct implementation.

In developing a community plan for the small city of Everett, Washington, Halprin used a scored downtown walk to establish a common language for the project. Full community involvement was required by the project grant, which was awarded to help Everett develop systems for future growth, to reverse the disintegration of its downtown and

corresponding suburban sprawl. During the walk, participants followed a prescribed course, exploring particular urban locations and
performing active tasks including drawing, evaluating what they saw,
and interacting with pedestrians. The shared experience of the walk
served as a catalyst for ideas and responses in a follow-up workshop.
A subsequent city-wide drive and helicopter ride expanded residents'
perspectives of local problems to a regional scale. Preliminary planning
objectives generated included provisions for open-space preservation,
pedestrian parks, location of future industrial complexes and various
densities of residential growth, pedestrian superblocks, better-coordi-
nated methods of traffic control, and plans for revitalization of downtown.

Of similar size and experiencing similar problems, the city of Char-
lottsville, Virginia, contacted Halprin to help them consider the course
of future community development and strategies for revitalizing
downtown. As a score for the project, Halprin stated: "Assume that it
has been proven that riding in automobiles causes impotence in males
—design your downtown to deal with this problem" (Chang, 1978).
From sketches of ideas offered in local workshops, the design team
developed a plan that quickly materialized into a completed pedestrian
street in the center of town. Less than three years after its completion,
the retail occupancy rate had risen from fifty to one hundred percent.

PROXEMIC BEHAVIOR

Proxemics is the study of how people unconsciously structure space in
their daily transactions. A notation system of proxemic behavior was
developed by Hall (1963), consisting of observations and a recording
technique for understanding human encounters. Background research in proxemics had been restricted to culturally specific behavior
and had not previously encompassed environmental and personality
variables, all of which are important in understanding environmental
behavior.

Proxemic behavior is a function of eight different dimensions and a
scale of measurement for each, including:

1. Postural-sex identifiers
2. Sociofugal–sociopetal orientation
3. Kinesthetic factors
4. Touch code
5. Retinal combinations
6. Thermal code
7. Olfaction code
8. Voice loudness scale

Each factor comprises a closed behavioral system that can be observed, recorded, and analyzed independently. An important initial operation in recording proxemic behavior is the determination of the sex and basic posture in which the standing, sitting, or prone position of each individual is coded by a number. Osmond (1959) uses the term sociofugal–sociopetal to describe spatial arrangements that push people apart or pull them together. These orientations increase or decrease interaction. The relationship between two bodies is recorded on a compass face with symbols corresponding to eight different positions. The kinesthetic code and notation system are based on what people can do with their arms, legs, and bodies. A seven-point scale codifies the contact–non-contact situations which vary significantly between cultures. Retinal combinations refer to where the subjects are looking and the degree to which eye contact is important. The heat code refers to changes in body temperature, while the olfactory code attempts to identify the presence of a body odor. Voice loudness is measured in seven degrees from silent to very loud and is judged against the standards of the observer.

This notation system was applied to the redesign of an insurance office in Sydney, Australia. An insurance society was interested in the effectiveness of applying personal satisfiers to the determination of an appropriate work environment. The project was conducted by Sloan (1970) as part of a postoccupancy evaluation study conducted by I. B. Fell Research Center (Purcell, Metcalfe, Thorne & Hall, 1972). Three departments were chosen for testing and observation and one department was chosen for office modification (Figure 4-10). Sloan observed and recorded over 2000 conversations within the accounts department alone, most of which took place within the work station and the majority within the department, suggesting a high degree of internal interaction. Based on Hall's notation system, people's activities in the immediate environment, in terms of interactions, positioning, and distancing, were observed and documented through the use of the data notation sheets shown in Figure 4-11.

In the office environment, many of the conversations occurred when individuals were seated at their desk. Business conversations were conducted at a closer range than social conversations. The results of observations indicated that the body orientation preferred by most workers during conversation is quite close and directly facing the conversant. Many of the interactions took place with only eighteen inches separating the conversants, with the two conversants directly facing each other for the majority of the time. In most conversations observed, both conversants used direct eye contact to reinforce communication, with very few indications of body or tactile contact. It was

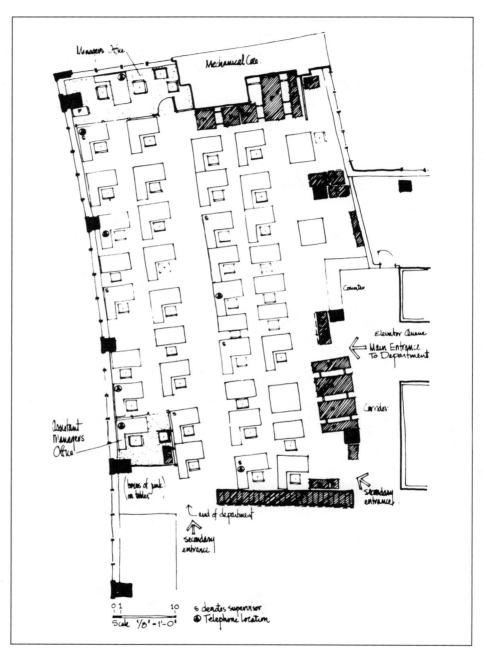

Figure 4-10: The arrangement of desks and working spaces in the department of Agency Accounts was typical of all major departments in the Sydney Cove office building. Desks were arranged in straight rows facing one direction. The department manager was located at the front of the rows, with a glass partition wall viewing the clerical area. Files were scattered around the perimeter of the space, and the department had three separate small entrances.

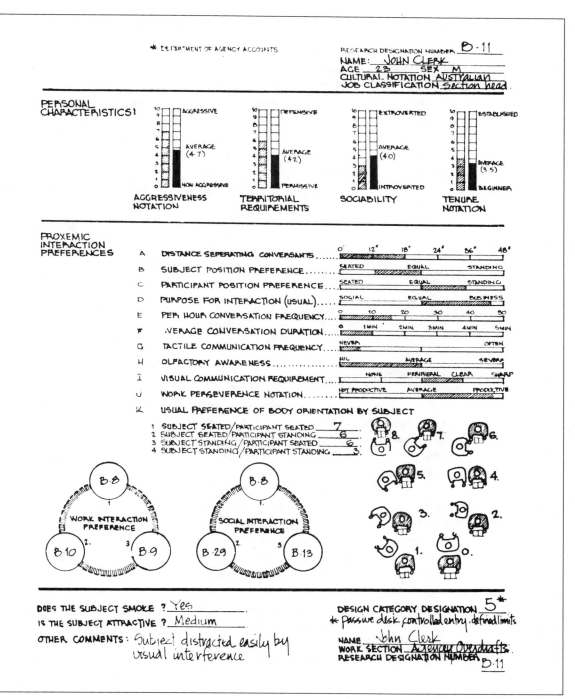

Figure 4-11: Notation data sheet for recording proxemic behavior in an office setting in Sydney, Australia (Reprinted from *Design Studies*, 1985, Vol. 6, No. 4. Henry Sanoff, editor).

observed that Australian business people seldom shake hands when they part company, and only during formal introductions will they shake hands when they are introduced.

Expressed territoriality in the workplace was noted, referring to 'he spacing and orientation of work stations or desks in order to prov ɔct against overexploitation of that part of the environment belonging to each worker. Quite often office workers will use charts and equipment such as typewriters to define their territory; many are bothered by external noise and visual activity as they attempt to work.

Observations charting the degree of friendliness of each office worker to others measured their degree of sociability, which was highly correlated with the frequency and duration of interactions. Office staff were also asked to indicate the people in the department with whom they most enjoyed working or conversing. From this the social leaders emerged. It was observed that requirements for territoriality, sociability, and aggressiveness varied widely from person to person. As a result, a categorization system was developed, based on the range of personal characteristics. In order to match the modification with the characteristics of the users, specific environmental requirements were identified to meet individual differences (Figure 4-12).

WAYFINDING AND NOTATION

Imageability has been associated with different environmental scales, ranging from cities to buildings, and describes an interaction between the environment and the observer (Lynch, 1960). For Lynch, the primary purpose of the mental image is to orient the person for purposeful mobility. Thus, the importance of being able to find one's way emerges as a dynamic factor in understanding people's mental images. Wayfinding requires complete involvement with the environment. Perceptual and cognitive processes are activated when people set out to reach particular destinations. Information is selectively extracted from the environment, and then interpreted, structured, and integrated into the existing body of knowledge.

Lynch stated that a mental image contained three components: identity, structure, and meaning. *Identity* related to people's ability to recognize environmental features. *Structure* implied the pattern of relations between certain places. Lynch also believed that the object must have *meaning* to the person. In support of these views, Downs and Stea (1973) stated that mental images consist of knowledge about the locations and attributes of the phenomena.

Wayfinding can be conceptualized as spatial problem solving, which incorporates information processing, decision making, and execution

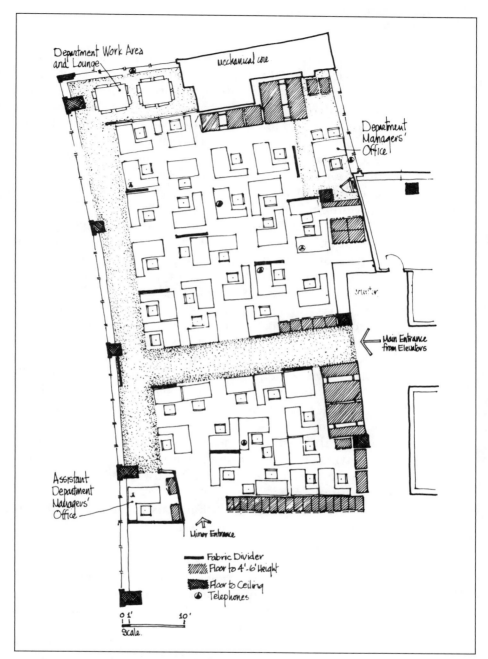

Figure 4-12: Desks were arranged in the Agency Accounts department to satisfy personal preferences and social requirements of each clerk. Cloth dividers were hung to subdivide the major space into smaller areas relating to work and social groups. The major aisle was carpeted, and the corner room (previously the manager's office) was made into a workroom for noisy equipment as well as a department lounge. Files were relocated to accommodate the location of those persons who used them. The files were also used to close minor entrances, giving definition of territory to the department. (Drawing: Sam Sloan).

(Passini, 1984). People are able to find their way through the physical environment by utilizing information concerning identification and location. The utilization of this information is, in turn, reflected by how the information is organized. Two methods of organizing information seem to emerge from the work of Stea (1969), Hart and Moore (1973), and Appleyard (1970). The first method is described as sequential, which requires the memorization of a sequence of events or a route (O'Keefe & Nadel, 1978). Another method implies the development of an understanding of the spatial relationships of the environment. An individual's mental image is usually composed of both of these organizational qualities, though Appleyard (1970) suggests that sequential images are a necessary prior development in the formulation of a spatial image. A person's image may be characterized as spatial in well-known parts of a building or town and as sequential in lesser known areas (Hunt, 1985).

Perceptual and cognitive phenomena, the various ways a person can relate to the spatial environment and to destinations, and memory and learning are all essential in explaining how people find their way (Passini, 1984). Unraveling the complex cord that people follow through the environment is essential in designing effective new systems.

The design of an efficient sign system, for example, would need to consider the sequences of decision making during a journey when information is sought. Notation systems for wayfinding link space and time through movement. In defining wayfinding as spatial problem solving, Passini proposed a notation system composed of two complementary parts, one reflecting the behavioral, the other the cognitive component.

The behavioral notation consists of the route chosen to a destination. This is indicated by a line with varying thickness according to the frequency of use (Figure 4-13). The route map reflects changes in direction which can be inferred to correspond to a series of decisions only if the route is relied upon as the only evidence. The behavioral notation is incomplete since it only records movement and locates decisions spatially.

A cognitive notation is an account of all decisions made, as well as the relations between those decisions. Passini refers to higher-order decisions, which is the information required to reach each decision in the diagram. The cognitive notation consists of a time sequence found on the vertical axis, combined with the horizontal sequence of decisions from general to specific that lead to a behavioral action. In a scenario illustrated by Passini, a person located on the ground floor of a shopping complex seeks out a toilet. The lines between decisions (D)

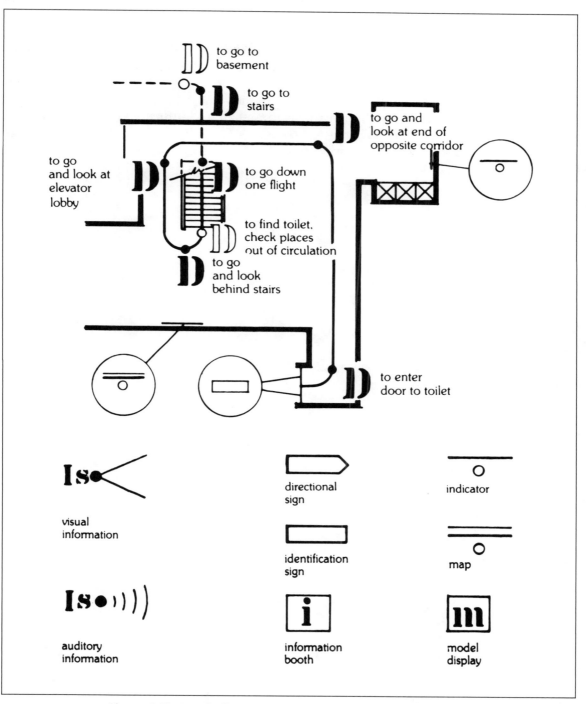

Figure 4-13: Wayfinding notation system (Drawing: Romedi Passini).

133

refer to the "in-order-to" relation, while the hatched surfaces cluster the decisions.

Each decision corresponds to units of information which are classified as sensory information (ls) that is readily perceived or memory information (lm), obtained during previous experiences. In Figure 4-13 (top), the information required to reach each decision in the diagram is recorded. Thus the cognitive notation explains the behavioral notation. The nature of the information is indicated by a set of symbols as shown in Figure 4-12 (bottom). Combined, these illustrations offer a shorthand description of a wayfinding episode.

5

ENVIRONMENTAL SIMULATION

Visual simulations are visual representations of something else and take many forms, such as photographs, maps, and models. The most up-to-date manual is Sheppard's *Visual Simulation* (1989), which is a user's guide for design and planning professionals. The Sheppard volume is an authoritative collection of case studies and guides for creating visual simulations. This section offers new perspectives and applications on scale models and computer graphics, augmenting other parts of this chapter which discuss maps, drawings, and photographs.

Visual simulations are used in a variety of ways as a design and as an analytic tool. Designers frequently use simulations in the development of a project, though clients and regulatory agencies may use simulations for review purposes. Simulations may also be used to elicit responses from the public and other user groups, since they are able to put the environmental conditions into an intended context and focus on a variety of issues.

Simulation research has dealt primarily with existing environments, where preferences or reactions were sought to different types of environments or scenes. Craik (1971) developed a model in which the test of validity is based on the similarity between responses to simulations and responses to reality. Studies of effectiveness of simulations have been conducted by Zube (1973), Acking and Küller (1973), and Sheppard (1988), who provide no clear consensus on levels of response similarity of simulations to reality. These studies have found differences between simulations and the corresponding built projects.

Different simulation media vary in level of detail, color characteristics, quality of reproduction, and conditions in which the simulation is depicted and in which it is seen, making it difficult to generalize from the results. Appleyard and Fishman (1977) and others believe that the more accurate the simulation is in characterizing an environment, the closer responses will be to those obtained in reality.

Based on a review of research and practical experience, Sheppard (1988) suggests several principles which can help to create valid and effective simulations.

Representative simulation: Simulations should reflect typical views that would normally be experienced by significant numbers of people. Viewpoints should be selected to represent conditions that closely resemble reality.

Accurate simulation: Accuracy, especially wherever experiential simulations are being used for visual assessment, may have a direct influence on the nature of the response. Simulations generally require some flexibility, should issues arise that were not easily predicted. Simulation accuracy may offer greater flexibility in applications.

Credible simulation: Simulations need to be believable if they are to communicate to users. Credibility is achieved by creating a realistic appearance. Kaplan (1977) suggests that people prefer realistic simulations because they are more accurate, though Appleyard and Fishman (1977) refer to this as "apparent realism."

Comprehensive simulation. The ease with which simulations are understood is also related to the credibility of the simulation. The medium for the simulation should be selected with the range of users in mind.

Bias-free simulation. Freedom from bias is the key factor of simulation validity (Appleyard & Fishman, 1977). Responses can be biased by the type of simulation, since assessments can be based on an individual's knowledge about aspects of the environment or personal feelings toward it. Simulations appropriate for one type of response may be misleading for another.

Ultimately, response equivalence can be assessed only after construction. As more evaluation of simulations is documented, it may be possible to predict response equivalence on the basis of past experience.

SPACES THAT CONNECT

Spaces that connect utilizes photographs to simulate destination-oriented walkways. This is an educational and research tool that seeks to identify the spatial characteristics that transmit cues which influence paths chosen by participants. Various spatial features of walkways signal observers to make movement decisions reflecting their spatial perceptions.

In research, using photographic images of spatial connectors allows analysis of features that influence people's walking behavior, perceptual differences that can be identified by different user groups, methods of classification of these perceptual features, and their relation to other environmental knowledge.

To increase awareness in an environmental education program, public school teachers were asked to participate in a three-step process of selecting a sequence of photographs corresponding to their destination goals. Since walking behavior takes people through a wide variety of indoor and outdoor passages, decisions about the appropriateness of a particular route over another is based on cues imbedded in the path features. Since the route chosen is often influenced by the purpose of the trip, whether hurried or leisurely, path features such as ground cover, amount of enclosure, path width, traffic, and visual variety all contribute to the decision process. This exercise proposed three typical situations people encounter in their walking behavior (Sanoff, Centeno & Göltsman, 1976). They were destination-oriented, but rushed; destination-oriented, but leisurely or exploratory; and leisurely, with no particular destination in mind.

Participants were given a set of twenty-three photographs and asked to select a set of pictures for each walking route and record the qualities of the spaces that influenced those decisions (Figure 5-1). Next, participants were asked to sort the photographs into groups of similar features and describe how they are similar. Finally, a series of origin-destination routes was identified, and participants organized the photographs into connector spaces for each situation.

Experience of the exercise was then used as a formal educational tool. Participating teachers were asked to develop exercises for their students using the new insights that they acquired. The language arts teacher developed community walks requiring students to construct paragraphs describing their walking experiences. The social studies teacher asked her students to examine the social history of the connecting spaces they visited. Geography students were asked to map their walking experiences, noting significant spatial features.

Figure 5-1: Options for spaces that connect (Photos: Greg Centeno & Henry Sanoff).

The use of photographs of connecting spaces enabled the development of personal comparisons between spatial features and judgments about the appearance and quality of particular walkways, corridors, and paths. Movement patterns and individual perceptions (Lynch & Rivkin, 1970) have also been the subject of studies in which responses have been recorded while actually moving through the urban environment. This approach, as well as the photographic simulation of spatial sequences, may likewise be useful for research purposes and as educational tools. The results of both approaches have proven to be an effective way of awakening people's interest in spatial characteristics of the environment.

SIMULATION BOOTH

The purpose of this project was to assess the feasibility of photographically simulating the patterns of user movement. Observed patterns of user movement in a museum were compared by Winkel and Sasanoff (1966), with patterns of user movement obtained in a simulated space. Color photographs of the interior of the museum were used to allow observers to report on how they would move through the museum and which exhibits they would view. Movement through the museum was selected as the user-behavior of interest because it represented the dynamics of a museum experience and because movement is influenced by the form and content of space.

The method of data gathering employed was *tracking* (Weiss & Boutourline, 1962). Plans of the main gallery of the museum were provided to each observer along with a stopwatch. The observers would track and record the movement of people in the space by drawing a line on the plan corresponding to the subjects' movement in the actual space. Additional user information was noted, including age, sex, and group behavior. Trackers attempted to remain unobtrusive and selected their subjects randomly at arbitrary time points at the museum entrance.

Once the tracking patterns of user behavior were analyzed, attention turned to the laboratory reconstruction of the real environment, where user behavior patterns could be compared with that of the actual patterns in the museum. The simulation consisted of projecting photographs on screens within a simulation booth. Photographs simulting the museum space were taken by establishing a five-foot square grid throughout the gallery space; eight exposures at 45-degree increments were photographed at eye level. Close-ups were also taken of the exhibition cases along the side walls. All photographs were taken when there were no people in the gallery.

The simulation booth consisted of three screens placed together with their edges touching. The screens were diagonally opposite the projector platform at a distance of eight and a half feet. The projectors were adjusted so that the rays of the two outer projectors crossed, making the axis of each projector perpendicular to its screen. The subjects were seated in front of the screens and were told by an experimenter to select the direction of travel as well as any particular exhibits they wished to see. The experimenter followed the observer's "trip" by marking it on a floor plan of the gallery along with notes of the particular exhibits seen. Two groups of subjects were also used for the simulation study. One volunteer group consisted of University of Washington college students and another group consisted of museum visitors who were randomly selected just before they entered the museum.

Composite maps were developed from the separate tracking maps to give an overview of paths which the subjects followed in the museum experience. The composite maps, however, did not provide complete information about the paths, and, in some cases, obscured the movement patterns. Since the composite maps only recorded movement patterns, they did not convey various experiences of the visitors nor the criteria they used for selecting particular paths.

Since the original goal of the project was to evaluate the experimental technique for the simulation of selected environments, it should be noted that the results confirmed that there are similarities between the real and simulated environments. The differences that occurred in the simulation were attributed to the fact that visitors in the booth were not subject to the fatigue normally experienced by museum visitors. As a result, a broader range of experiences was selected by the simulation booth subjects. Also, the slides in the simulation restricted the viewers' ability to scan the environment extensively. Thus the degree to which a comprehensive image of a space can be achieved was a factor requiring further study. Furthermore, the ability of the museum visitor to orient himself in the space is denied the observer in the simulation booth. After the simulation trip was completed, the subjects were interviewed about their reactions to the simulation booth and the museum. Comments from the group indicated that some were uncertain about which parts of the gallery they had visited.

A testing device that would have allowed the simulation booth subjects greater opportunities to scan the environment is video scanning. Video touring might reveal patterns of movement which are in closer congruence with actual path behavior.

SIMULATION MODELS

A modeling kit representing building components was developed for a Canadian cooperative program (Bentz, 1980) to engage families in visualizing selections of house designs chosen from a variety of sources (Figure 5-2).

The kit was designed with a black, unreflective acrylic base that was grooved to receive polystyrene sheet components. The wall components included openings for doors and windows. An added level of realization was achieved by using a clear acrylic sheet with a grid of milled grooves to allow the user to see what has been modeled on the level beneath. The kit components in 1:16 scale allowed the pieces to be manipulated easily while producing a manageable finished model.

Participants have photographed their models for future reference, but more commonly made sketches, altered them, or made other notations to record changes that resulted from working with the kit. Users of the kit reported adjustments in their perception of their designs. Most commonly, they thought room sizes to be larger than they actually were. This new understanding of "real" house space accounted for the considerable number of changes made.

a

Figure 5-2: Three-dimensional scale model constructed by inexperienced partipants (a) Partition wall decisions; (b) Placement of furnishings; (c) Completed panel model (Photos: Bruce Bentz).

Fig. 5-2 continued

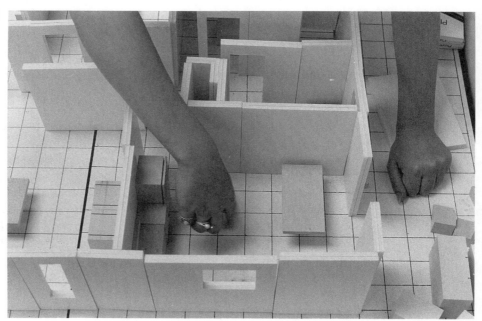

b

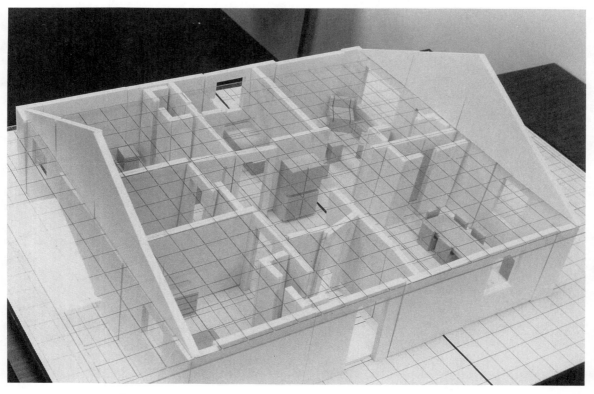

c

Three-dimensional Simulation Achieving coincidence between intended and resulting design and optimal "fit" between users and designed environments are standing concerns in architecture. The public participation approach to design in particular seeks to establish direct links between client needs and desires and the interpretive work of the architect by including prospective users in the design process. In spite of the number and variety of professional–client collaborations and the literature produced which attempts to describe their contributions and interactions, little attention has been given to the transfer from verbal to graphic representations of space and to communication of information between the architect and the client (Lawrence, 1981). Typically, resulting spaces are different, and less satisfactory, than anticipated, and changes are prescribed for a completed project or for the participation process used.

The Laboratory of Architectural Experimentation (L.A.E.) at the Ecole Polytechique Federale in Lausanne, Switzerland, was instituted to allow a more tangible appreciation of design intentions during the design process. Modular plastic blocks are used in constructing full-scale mock-ups of prospective houses (Figure 5-3), permitting testing of the three-dimensional implications of two-dimensional plans. Virtually all angles and curved surfaces can be achieved using the three types of blocks, which are dimensioned on a 10-cm module (Matti and von Meiss, 1982). Simple, prestressed post and beam assemblies can be produced using the same blocks and specially developed hardware. The walls can support light loads and can be braced or reinforced if desired. An intermediary floor, equipped with various types of artificial ceiling lighting, can be introduced using a vertically adjustable platform.

To lend realism to the designs, door and window frames of any dimension can be installed, podiums can be stacked to simulate subtle changes in level, and an adjustable stair can be added. A carpentry shop equipped with saws and other tools can produce special elements, and interior furnishings can be added to complete spatial settings.

The L.A.E. was initially conceived as a teaching tool for architecture students at the Ecole Polytechnique. Rather than relying on untested mental images of what they design, or being "taught" the consequences of their decisions, students can actually build and experience what they draw. For more senior students and researchers, the laboratory provides the opportunity to isolate the test variables in the environment and their relationships to human behavior. The facility has proved useful and insightful to practicing architects, clients, and public agencies in designing new or modified environments. Especially when technologically complex spaces or repetitive units are contemplated, the opportunity to simulate and alter a project can result in considerable savings in cost and user dissatisfaction.

Figure 5-3: Stages in the design-by-simulation process (Photos: Rod Lawrence).

FULLSCALE MODELWORKSHOP

The Fullscale Modelworkshop was established in Denmark to create a forum for residents, professionals, and students to discuss research and to develop housing from shared experiences and understanding of the connection between living patterns and the enclosing environment. These discussions culminate in the creation of three-dimensional and fullscale models.

The Danish workshop is distinctive in being mobile and flexible. Models of up to several stories can be built anywhere in the country where a large space is available (Figure 5-4). This on-site mobility increases the potential for user-oriented housing solutions. The establishment of the Modelworkshop is seen as a link in the development of methods used for the improvement of existing housing and in the planning of new housing types.

Figure 5-4: Interior of Fullscale Model workshop (Photo: Peder Dueland Mortensen).

Numerous fullscale model projects were carried out in towns and housing estates in Denmark and abroad, where improvements of the existing environment were planned or new housing initiatives were taken. The models have given professionals and users a common language and have involved the users directly in development work. Debate and evaluation can occur, and suggestions for change can be realized and tested immediately on the models. Not incidentally, the Modelworkshop has given residents in public housing confidence in their own creative abilities.

LUND SIMULATOR

The Lund Simulator (Janssens & Küller, 1986) is used to simulate and evaluate planned physical environments in model form. An overhead suspension system permanently mounted in the ceiling supports a television camera with an inverted periscope. A steering system controls camera movement in three directions. The model is placed on a table under the suspension system (Figure 5-5).

Figure 5-5: Simulator at Lund (Photo: Rikard Küller).

In another room, the picture taken by the television camera is transmitted to a television screen in front of the operator, who controls movement of the periscope with a steering wheel and a speed pedal (described as a "relatoscope"). Several television monitors can be connected for other observers, and all pictures can be recorded on videotape.

The simulator can also be used as a research tool. Subjects' eye movements, for example, can be recorded in connection with a particular sequence of the run through the model. Models of interiors and exteriors can be presented realistically with a detailed study of subjective evaluation and objective eye movement of the viewer.

The range of applications of the Lund Simulator is considerable. Participant observers, including designers, building committees, and the general public have used the system to understand and foresee the impact of plans for construction or rebuilding in the real environment. One project dealt with model options for a highway planned to intersect a sensitive residential area. Another study compared different design solutions for the completion of a town square, using interchangeable model parts. To portray a project adequately by means of television, the models require detailed depiction of parts of the environment (Figure 5-6).

COMPUTER SIMULATION

Computers are a new tool that have descended on design researchers and professionals and are changing the way graphic information is generated and used. As a simulation tool, computers can approach

Figure 5-6: Modelscope photographs (Photos: Rikard Küller).

modeling with software that utilizes lines, surfaces, shapes, or all three. Current graphics software can accurately represent how a proposed building's spaces and shapes will be organized, colored, textured, lighted, and supported. The most basic viewing display shows a parallel line image of objects in space. These wire frame images can be enhanced by surface shading, automatically shading, or painting to make the wire frame look more realistic. In addition to individual views, sequential views can be created around and through buildings. Walk-throughs can be displayed in rapid sequence to simulate real-time sequences as well as step-by-step sequences.

As the tool for creating and managing three-dimensional architectural models, CADD is a database manager which structures how information is entered, manipulated, displayed, and stored. The new visualization technology takes CADD data and combines it with environmental images and material swatches to express the visual relationship between proposed structures and existing conditions. While CADD technology enables the generation of perspective drawings, it does not create a realistic depiction of proposed buildings or environmental settings. Advanced computer technology has considerable ability to mimic reality. In the effort to enhance the interaction of the user and computer, special components have been developed to construct "artificial reality" (Foley, 1987).

The display monitor in most common workstations permits a viewing distance of two feet, with a visual field that covers less than 20 percent of the actual range of one eye. Displays that fill the visual field give the observer a sense of being part of a scene, rather than being on the outside looking in. Hence, wall-size projections of computer screens would help to imbed the observer in an artificial reality.

The most advanced method for improving realism is the head-mounted display. The display can facilitate depth perception through the stereoscopic effect of providing each eye with a slightly offset view of the same image. Using an electronic sensor that registers head position, the display provides additional depth cues as the background shifts when the observer changes his or her eye position. The sensor allows the observer to scan an artificial panorama in response to turning of the head.

The electronic sensor that registers head position and orientation was developed for NASA by the Polhemus Navigation Sciences division of the McDonald Douglass Corporation. Eye trackers were used to gather data on how people read and examine pictures. The eye trackers bounce a beam of light off the eye, and the direction in which the light is reflected indicates where the user is looking. Wall-size screens, head mounted displays, position sensors and eye trackers can improve the credibility of an artificial reality by broadening the visual field.

Currently available, off-the-shelf technology developed by the Land Development Laboratory (Welsh, 1988) provides a visualization system that incorporates video imaging, CADD computer rendering, and survey technologies to produce photorealistic images depicting proposed projects combined with actual images of the intended site (Figure 5-7).

Figure 5-7: Computer simulation of proposed building on the site (Photos: Land Development Laboratory).

By taking accurate measurements of the proposed building site, video-taping the existing environment, and then combining these raster images with fully rendered CADD models of the proposed building, precise perpsective graphics can be generated. The technology can be used to make effective presentations to general audiences, allowing analysis of the visual impact of a proposed project.

The site visits consist of measurement of the area, using standard surveying techniques, and making a videotape of the area. When the 3D-model information has been compiled, the material properties of the building, such as building material, texture of surfaces, and transparency are specified. Various light sources and vantage points, and pathways along which the viewer will travel, are defined and positioned within the CADD file, enhanced by shadow casting and environmental mapping. The result of this work is generally a 512-line videotape of about four to seven minutes in length. Site movement, including people walking down the street, is invoked by cutting a window into the CADD image of the building in order to play a piece of videotape "through the window." Images are combined and recorded on tape to simulate action outside the building.

Animation is the term that refers to the dynamic representation of the environment. An animated presentation, by the Archsoft Group (Neeley, 1989), of the design of several buildings adjacent to a freeway consisted of a sequence beginning with the site seen from the air. The animation then dropped down to the freeway level and showed the site and buildings as they would be viewed coming from the off ramp and driving up to the parking lot. Animated views from above can show shadow patterns, and a variety of colors and materials. Three-dimensional simulations have also been used by Design Workshop, Inc. (Metzger, 1989), to establish databases of cities that can be updated over time to show the evolution of the city and to evaluate proposed projects.

COMPUTERIZED USER FLOW PATTERNS

A security evaluation of a United States embassy building performed by Heimsath and Heimsath (1989) used CADD graphics to study and structure user flow patterns. User groups were differentiated into five categories, which were subsequently classified as *served* and *service users.* Each user group was followed through a series of typical events or user episodes. A user may go through a series of episodes, for example, upon entering the embassy. These might include: (1) determining place image, (2) confirming place, (3) transition, (4) acknowledgment, and (5) interaction.

To illustrate this process, "the visitor arrives at the embassy at the main gate, passes through a security check, proceeds down an open walk to the chancery (confirming place), enters lobby (transition), checks with the receptionist and the Marine guard (acknowledgment), then enters the consular area (interaction)." The collection of repetitive episodes constituted the user sequence. When the user sequences occurred over regular intervals, they constituted a user pattern. The patterns were then graphically represented as shown in Figure 5-8, for two entry conditions.

Three-dimensional CADD graphics were used in a detailed examination of the new embassy lobby, plotting undesirable cross patterns of circulation. An alternate lobby arrangement was proposed as a result clarifying various user performance requirements.

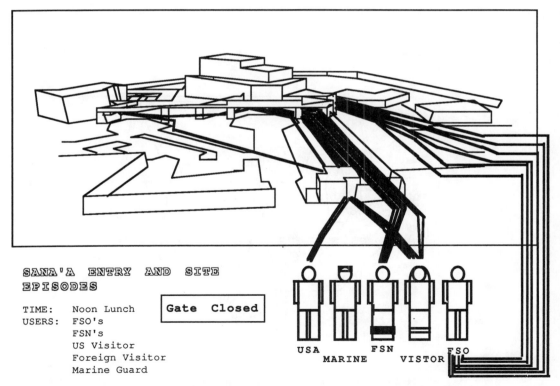

SANA'A ENTRY AND SITE
EPISODES

TIME: Noon Lunch
USERS: FSO's
         FSN's
         US Visitor
         Foreign Visitor
         Marine Guard

Gate Closed

USA   MARINE   FSN   VISTOR   FSO

Figure 5-8a: Computer simulation of user flow process (Drawing: Clovis Heimsath).

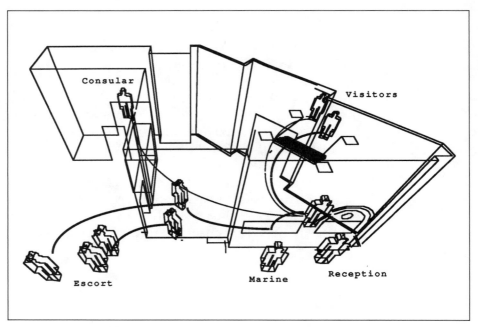

Figure 5-8b: Existing lobby (Drawing: Clovis Heimsath).

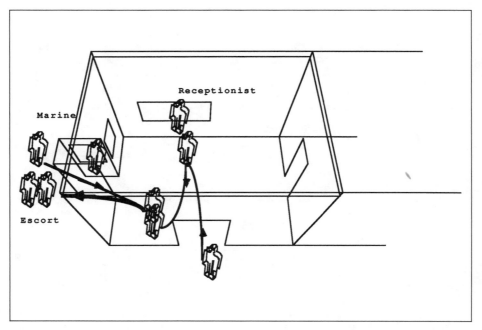

Figure 5-8c: Alternative lobby design improves escort clarity (Drawing: Clovis Heimsath).

VIRTUAL ENVIRONMENTAL DISPLAY

Recent advances in supercomputer applications hold special promise for the design and experience of simulated architectural environments. Artificial realities allow the user to interact with the computer in an intuitive and direct way and to increase the number of interactions per unit of time. The ultimate objective of artificial-reality research is to develop a simulated environment that seems as "real" as the reality it depicts (Foley, 1987).

Artificial realities have three components: imagery, behavior, and interaction. Realistic visual imagery enables the user to interpret information presented by the computer. The images may represent real objects, such as buildings, and they behave the way the objects they represent would behave. The user interacts with an artificial reality in the same way as he interacts with the three-dimensional world: by moving, pointing, and picking things up, by talking and observing from many different angles.

Developed at NASA's Ames Research Center in Moffett Field, California, for use in automated space stations, a head-mounted, wide-angle stereoscopic display system allows users to explore a 360-degree synthesized or remotely sensed environment. This display can facilitate depth perception in much the same way as a Vu-Master achieves its stereoscopic effect: each eye is provided with a slightly offset view of the same image. Inside the VIVED (Virtual Visual Environmental Display) helmet, monochromatic liquid crystal display screens present to each eye a binocular field of view which is updated with changes in head motion. Imagery in full motion parallax and perspective is delivered as the user moves through the virtual environment. Imagery appears to surround the user in three-dimensional space and allows exploration in real time from multiple viewpoints. The effect is achieved with the aid of a sensor that registers head position and orientation. Because the sensor recognizes gross head movements, the user can experience the illusion of scanning an artificial panorama as he turns his head. Using commercial and custom video mixing and switching equipment, multiple, interchangeable images can be overlaid on a common background.

Corresponding three-dimensional sound technology can be used to enhance overall situational awareness, and to provide information and spatial cues for objects or events both within or outside of the operator's field of view. The motion-tracking system updates sound cues through headphones to maintain contact with the changing field of imagery.

Light-weight "Datagloves" used in conjunction with the VIVED helmet allow the operator to pick up and manipulate objects in the display environment. Records of arm, hand, and finger shape and position are tracked to coordinate tactile experience with visual and auditory. VPL Research, Inc., the small California company which developed the glove, is using Dataglove principles in a Datasuit to cover the entire human body.

SIMULATION IN CONTEXT

Gaming is an approach to problem solving that engages a real-life situation compressed in time so that the essential characteristics of the problem are open to examination. The technique is particularly appealing because it permits learning about the process of change in a dynamic environment requiring periodic decisions. Essentially, we are identifying a complex problem and abstracting its essence, a process referred to as simulation. Games help sharpen perceptions, and can provide insights into situations so familiar that their characteristics are not perceived.

The semiotics game was designed by Bonta (1979) to explore identity recognition and meaning attributed to building types. The premise of the game is that the environment consists of buildings whose intended meaning has long been forgotten. Their successful endurance can best be explained as an acceptance of what the buildings are, and not what their designers intended them to be.

Semiotics is basically used to identify stereotypes and cliches held by the group of players. It can be played by up to fifteen people. Each player is assigned a building type from a list containing such terms such as *residential, industrial, religious,* and so on. There is also a list of adjectives which include words such as *rational, functional, bold* and *modern.* One adjective is assigned to each player, who must then select two additional and compatible adjectives. Players then receive a kit of wood blocks of various shapes and sizes and are asked to design a building that corresponds to the type and adjectives assigned (Figure 5-9). The completed designs are then scored by each player who selects four adjectives that best describe the design solution. Players then have scores as both designers and interpreters.

SIMULATION GAMES FOR INFORMATION COLLECTION

Most researchers and designers know that information collected about existing and proposed environments through conventional survey techniques is limited by the preconceptions of the researcher who formulates the study and the narrowness of structured communication. The desire to overcome those limitations, by allowing a special group

Figure 5-9: Various buildings types designed by participants using wood blocks (Photo: Juan Bonta).

of subjects to respond more freely and effectively about aspects of an environment under study, led researchers in the Canberra Bureau of Transportation Economics to develop a simulation game to assess the effectiveness of efforts to adapt the city's transit system for disabled persons (Faulkner, 1985). The study attempted to understand the travel behavior of disabled people and problems they experienced in using the existing system, suggesting modifications that might be made.

The Disabled Persons Transportation Game included a preliminary survey of participants, in addition to setting up and using the gameboard. The survey provided background information about the nature of each person's disability and its effect on mobility. Each participant then positioned flags and other markers representing regular (that is, at least once a month) travel destinations on the gameboard map. Information was requested about each designated destination, including purpose, frequency, mode of travel, assistance required, difficulties encountered, and other stops incorporated in each trip. Before the actual game began, the participants were asked to indicate destinations of any trips which they would like to make but couldn't, and to explain the impediments.

The game presented players with alternative forms of transport, constraining their choices by regulating the number and value of counters with which each trip was to be purchased. First, each person was presented with 30 percent fewer counters than would be required to maintain the existing pattern of travel. Then, an additional allowance of thirty counters (about $12) per week was provided. Finally, all trips were made free. Observing the process of coping with both restrictive and unlimited budgets provided a means of establishing the significance of economic factors in travel, of indicating the priorities and alternative strategies of the participants, and of understanding real behavioral factors corresponding to each decision.

Results revealed that 40 percent of the participants had ready access to a private car, traveled frequently, and did not wish to change their travel habits with different modes of transportation. Of the remaining 60 percent who had limited access to a car and were unable to travel independently, 16 percent were satisfied with their level of travel and did not wish to make changes; 27 percent were willing and able to resolve any travel restrictions with the extra funds provided during the game; and the remaining 17 percent were unable to solve their transportation problems due to their social and psychological nature. Economics, then, was a significant factor in limiting travel for only a portion of the participants, while others were restricted by feelings of self-consciousness, inadequacy, inferiority, lack of companionship, and reactions of drivers and fellow passengers.

Conductors of the study felt that the gaming technique was especially successful in allowing participants to visualize, remember, and record more accurately their travel patterns, and in providing a reference base for clarifying questions and responses. Actual and alternative transportation systems were more easily presented and understood. Moreover, because of the novelty of the game itself and the use of a model, participants' interest and participation were better sustained than in a more conventional survey situation.

The researchers acknowledged, however, that developing the game involved more pretesting and experimentation than is typical of conventional questionnaires, and using it restricted the size of the study due to the amount of personal participation required by the interviewers. Data produced by the technique was more qualitative in nature and less amenable to statistical inference. Weighing its benefits and limitations, the researchers recommend the use of simulation games as a supplement to other types of information gathering.

HOUSING LAYOUT GAME

The Houses Game developed by Bishop and Russell (1984), introduces participants to a variety of environmental decisions related to housing layout. Each player has the opportunity to propose solutions as well as to evaluate other ideas from the group. The Houses Game can be used to consider both urban and rural sites to engage participants in trade-offs of items which cannot all be achieved in full. Its primary purpose is to expose the way personal and group values influence the selection of environments, calling into question attempts by any group to make decisions on behalf of others.

The game consists of twelve house templates, each with a private back garden, and an evaluation kit. Participants seek to develop a layout that is *attractive, easy to live in,* and as *cheap* as possible. Guidelines are provided for the criteria of cheapness (Figure 5-10), although

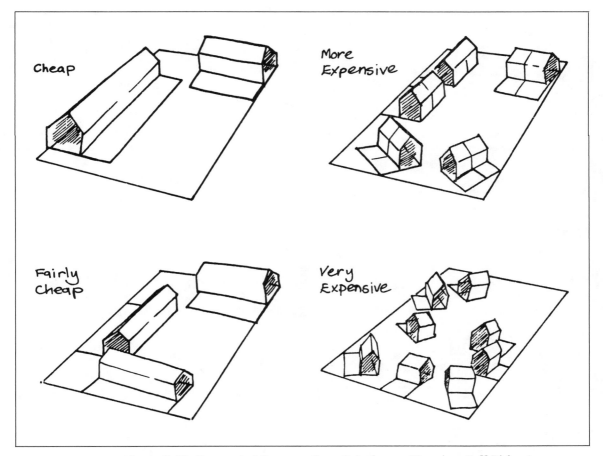

Figure 5-10: Economical factors reflected site layout (Drawing: Jeff Bishop).

attractiveness is regarded as a personal judgment. The main rules for organizing a layout consist of *accessibility between houses, sunlight in every back garden, parking for each house,* and *public open space.* Participants evaluate each others' solutions using the scoring template.

Modifications to the Houses Game can include the use of a real local site, variations in density, and the addition of community facilities. The needs of various client groups such as the elderly, single people, young couples, the disabled, or a commune can also be examined.

6

PLANNING AND DESIGN

The case studies which follow illustrate ways in which various processes for community participation in design were tailored and combined in planning more comprehensive or complex environments. All projects began with exercises to raise participants' awareness of design issues, empowering them to make informed decisions and to respond knowledgeably to preliminary and final proposals. In establishing links between shared community goals and design solutions, working groups were required to make consensus decisions, arguing persuasively for their ideas. In coming to group agreement about a limited number of objectives, participation of all members in discussion was promoted, and the passive and inhibiting tendency of win/lose voting was avoided.

Essential long-term commitment to community projects was established through a direct citizen involvement in the earliest stages of problem or need identification. Making those affected active partners in directing change, rather than eventual recipients of professionals' determinations, increases the likelihood that interest and advocacy will be maintained until and after the desired results are achieved.

Each project employs the use of visual images to establish a dialogue between professionals and community members. The techniques are designed for a variety of purposes, including increasing participant awareness, providing information, promoting discussion about design alternatives, and facilitating decision making.

159

GOAL SETTING IN DESIGN

My experiences in the town of Gibson illustrate the ways in which research techniques can be used to make connections between awareness, perception, decision making, and implementation. This cotton farming town began in the first half of the nineteenth century when a stagecoach rest stop was established at Noah Gibson's General Store. Further commercial expansion occurred with the building of the railroad. Gibson's development peaked in the 1940's, but rapidly declined after World War II, when technology advances in machinery, power, and chemicals were made available to farmers. Since the 1940's a net out-migration occurred in Gibson, leveling off in the 1970's to its present population of 502 people. The existing business sector of the county could be characterized as growing, undiversified industrial, supported by a small service sector. The low-density population, with low purchasing power, is willing to commute long distances for low to moderate paying jobs.

Gibson's own business sector could be characterized as untapped and undeveloped in employment and purchasing potential. Local cultural characteristics and economics would play an important role in the future of Gibson's business sector, since citizens are accustomed to shopping twenty miles away. The primary users of Gibson's downtown are the elderly and blacks who do not have the inclination or transportation to take a twenty-mile round trip.

In assessing Gibson's potential for residential and business growth, local businessmen and town officials sought assistance in community organization. In less than one year a nonprofit community development organization was formed in order to distribute and allocate funds received from private grants and public monies.

While the citizens and the newly formed community development corporation were interested in expanding their services, they still wanted to retain their small-town character. They requested my design and planning assistance for a revitalization strategy to give life back to the declining town.

Like every town, Gibson has its own special personality. The unique combination of elements such as the size of the town, the people who live there, and its buildings, all contribute to the town's identity. Quite often the character of a town is taken for granted or unnoticed until successive changes call attention to its new face. Gibson is unique in that it has not gone through the building alterations so common in neighboring communities. As the process of deciding upon Gibson's future began, it seemed desirable to have the residents renew their acquaintance with the town.

In order to begin a dialogue about the problems and resources of the downtown, a Gibson town walk was proposed. Specific paths were designated for townspeople to walk and record their observations and impressions. Maps were distributed at the local shops depicting nodal points in the town where residents were asked to make a special note of the occurrences they observed. Children, too, were involved in describing their feelings about Gibson. All school teachers were asked to conduct exercises in the classroom, encouraging children to sketch their favorite places as well as desired new features for the town.

Since any town revitalization effort in the United States requires community support, an open invitation was extended to residents of the community to attend a planning workshop. Gibsonians would not only have to invest in the growth of the town, but they would be involved in changes in the way the downtown would function. The children's drawings covered the walls of the community meeting room where their first workshop took place.

Ten vacant buildings in the downtown area represented 30 percent of the usable building inventory. Since many of the owners of the vacant properties did not reside in Gibson, it was important not only to find appropriate uses for these vacant buildings, but to exert pressure on the absentee owners to sell the properties. Thus, it was decided that finding a use for the vacant buildings was an important objective that would require special community support, particularly if the residents were to have a stake in reviving the downtown area.

A workshop strategy was developed to provide community participants with the opportunity to engage in a process of choosing appropriate uses for vacant buildings. We believed that each participant should have an equal voice in decision making in an atmosphere of open communication. To achieve this goal we developed a workshop package that included a base map of the town, a set of activity charts that defined a variety of public and private uses for the vacant buildings, and a set of building survey sheets describing the size and condition of each building and corresponding graphic symbols for each use. Each participant received a set of these materials for use during the workshop, which was designed for a period of three hours.

Twenty Gibsonians voluntarily participated in the Downtown Workshop held at the old railroad depot. Although this may appear to be a small group, it generated a variety of viewpoints. Three workgroups were randomly identified, with one designer acting as a facilitator for each team. Small groups were used to assure that everyone would have an opportunity to contribute his or her ideas in the planning process. In order to create an informal atmosphere among the participants, a get-acquainted exercise was conducted in which people asked questions of one another and then introduced each other to the group. This technique promoted response and self-disclosure of initial perceptions, even between participants who already knew each other.

The initial step in the process required each member to develop a downtown plan by placing his or her individual activity choices on a score sheet corresponding to the base map (Figure 6-1). Next, each score sheet representing individual choices was reviewed by the group. We requested that each group arrive at a consensus plan and avoid reaching a solution by voting. Consensus decision making encourages all viewpoints to be expressed and provides the opportunity for people to learn from each other. Voting usually inhibits the free flow of ideas and often results in alienation of community members. The consensus

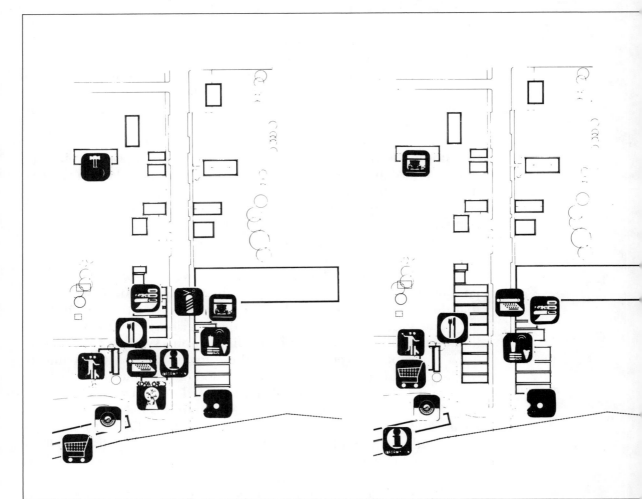

Figure 6-1: Activity location options developed by three Gibson community groups.

approach constructively involved the participants in a collaborative planning process where positions were won or lost by the persuasiveness of the argument. People whose positions were not popular still believed that the process was fair, since all viewpoints were heard by the team members.

When each work group arrived at an acceptable plan, all participants reviewed the three proposals for the use of vacant properties in downtown Gibson. Each plan was presented by a community member, and major disagreements were discussed in order to advance the prevailing viewpoints. The two controversial issues were the best location for a restaurant and the disposition of an old barn situated in the downtown area. Two groups proposed that the vacant fire station was the best

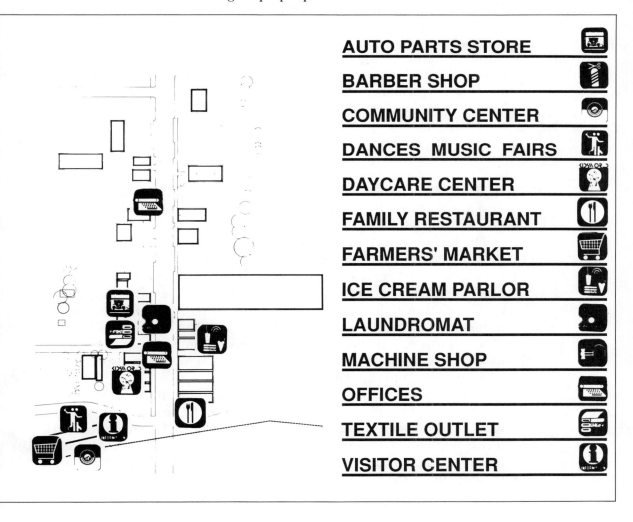

AUTO PARTS STORE

BARBER SHOP

COMMUNITY CENTER

DANCES MUSIC FAIRS

DAYCARE CENTER

FAMILY RESTAURANT

FARMERS' MARKET

ICE CREAM PARLOR

LAUNDROMAT

MACHINE SHOP

OFFICES

TEXTILE OUTLET

VISITOR CENTER

location for the restaurant because it afforded ample parking space and provided the possibility of outdoor eating. Their position was not easily contested; after considerable site analysis by the planning team, the decision was made to locate the restaurant in the fire station which was owned by the town and donated to the local community development corporation. With the aid of a private grant, a member of the community agreed to assume responsibility for managing the restaurant, which is presently in operation.

Another important decision made at the group meeting was the need for a community center. All groups identified the vacant railroad station as the most suitable location, particularly since the history of the town centered on the depot. Now, some trains make occasional freight stops, but most trains only pass through Gibson without stopping. The re-use of the railroad depot, which was donated by the railroad company to the town, was designated as the first priority for implementation at the community workshop. The planning team discussed the various uses of this facility, which would include dancing, musical performances, a library, and a meeting hall. The depot has already been renovated and refurbished with the help of grants, donated materials, and volunteer labor from local citizens.

Another activity generated by the workshop was workdays. Clean-up days were held on a regular basis to maintain neighborhood yards and public places. Downtown clean-up consisted of trash removal and clearing of vacant lots. The increased sense of town identity and pride developed through the clean-ups led to the construction of a new downtown park.

The initial workshop, then, was the beginning of a number of events held in Gibson. Because small towns engage their residents in a number of social and service organizations, not all people wished to or had time to be involved in community workshops. Nevertheless, it was evident that overall community involvement from all segments of the population, particularly in construction projects, was especially high. Much of this was attributed to continuous communication by the local newspaper, inviting the residents' participation in ways consistent with their interests and capabilities.

In a period of one year, much of Gibson's potential for development was realized through a community development process which began with a rediscovery of the town's worth, and moved systematically towards implementation of a number of community projects. Although there had been several previous attempts to upgrade the town through various master plans, the direct involvement of the community through the use of visual techniques was instrumental in helping to create physical changes in a town that had been dormant for the past forty years.

KNOWLEDGE OF EMERGING ENVIRONMENTAL PRESERVATION STRATEGIES (KEEPS)

This goal-based, user-oriented plan was developed for a small town, involving working groups of residents in a process enabling planning decisions for a twenty-year period of time. In the initial stages, key planning concepts were transferred to the townspeople, who subsequenty assumed decision-making responsibilities. The process was initiated by identifying environmental qualities, formulating community goals, and matching the appropriate strategies to the goals.

Environmental qualities refer to a town's unique characteristics, which can be identified through an awareness walk, video or slide show, or, in this instance, a sequence of drawings dramatically illustrating the process of change. Three drawings depicted the evolution of a town or neighborhood, as a result of progress or planning neglect (Figure 6-2). Drawing 1 represented the past; drawing 2 portrayed the present; and drawing 3 suggested a future appearance if action by the community was not taken. Although the scenarios are hypothetical, they represent familiar phenomena for people residing in such towns as well as for those who are embarking upon revitalization schemes.

Participation begins with noting qualities that were lost or those that should be retained, and then sharing viewpoints with each other. Next, participants select from a prepared list of goal statements four that would promote the desired qualities. The individual lists are pooled, and each group is required to propose four statements that have received consensus after individuals have forcefully lobbied for their individual choices.

From the strategies list, participants select four methods for implementing each goal. Again, the individual lists are pooled and discussed before a final group selection is made. The combined results of all working groups provide a framework for future discussions. The process takes participants from an awareness of the situation to a plan for action.

The model was used in the town of Murfreesboro, North Carolina, where members of the local historical society participated in the development of a plan for their historic district (Sanoff, 1979). The planning strategy involved the identification of a number of concerns and the organization of community members into groups working with planners and designers in identifying qualities of importance to the area, goals, and implementation strategies (Figure 6-3). In addition to considering general issues such as visual quality and historic district image, the project included dividing the area into subdistricts and developing similar work sheets for use by community residents.

STRATEGIES

—Encourage property owners to increase property maintenance.
—Encourage civic organizations to clean up, or maintain sites.
—Offer preliminary architectural services to businesses and individuals interested in developing sites.
—Encourage private planting programs.
—Move some historically significant building to infill a key unoccupied site.
—Encourage pedestrian activities in key areas by petitioning for walkway improvement programs.
—Contact other organizations that have initiated similar projects for advise.
—Have an area wide 'planting day.'
—Develop detailed design guidelines to maintain a consistent area image.
—Organize for bulk purchase of materials.
—Acquire public agency support.
—Encourage the demolition of buildings that are hopelessly beyond repair.
—Use local media sources to obtain issue visibility.
—Look into the possibility of federal and state grants.
—Lobby for zoning changes which can insure the implementation of your goals.
—Purchase and restore key buildings and sites to 'period authenticity'.
—Sponsor continuing area wide 'clean up day' programs.
—Identify and evaluate historically significant buildings and sites.
—Purchase, rehabilitate, and adaptively reuse significant buildings and sites.
—Develop property easement programs and standards.
—Put utilities underground.
—Purchase, rehabilitate and sell.
—Purchase, rehabilitate and rent.
—Control of outdoor advertising.
—Develop a revolving fund.
—Tree planting and maintenance of publically owned property.

GOALS

—Preserve historically significant sites, landmarks, objects, and buildings.
—More public and private involvement in decisions which could alter the character of the area.
—Heightened public awareness to the area's unique physical character.
—Optimal use, or re-use of sites in the area.
—Preservation of the neighborhood's visual characteristics.
—Influence public and private investment for the good of the area.
—Neighborhood development which is compatible with the long range objectives for town development.
—Public awareness to the area's historic resources.
—Preservation of neighborhood social cohesiveness.
—Maintenance and upgrading of properties.
—Increased public participation in the development of the area.
—Influence neighborhood improvement programs in other parts of town.
—Control of growth and development in the area.

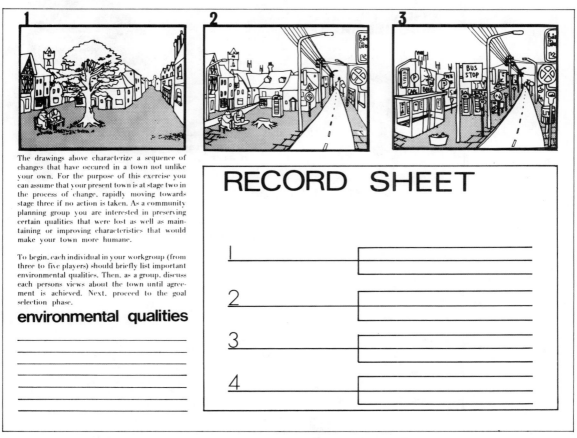

The drawings above characterize a sequence of changes that have occured in a town not unlike your own. For the purpose of this exercise you can assume that your present town is at stage two in the process of change, rapidly moving towards stage three if no action is taken. As a community planning group you are interested in preserving certain qualities that were lost as well as maintaining or improving characteristics that would make your town more humane.

To begin, each individual in your workgroup (from three to five players) should briefly list important environmental qualities. Then, as a group, discuss each persons views about the town until agreement is achieved. Next, proceed to the goal selection phase.

environmental qualities

RECORD SHEET

1

2

3

4

Figure 6-2: A sequence of drawings characterizing change in a community, used to establish guidelines for desired environmental qualities, goals, and implementation strategies (From Henry Sanoff, *Designing with Community Participation,* Van Nostrand Reinhold, 1978).

C
VISUAL QUALITY—MURFREESBORO

goals related to area

🖐 ADD & DELETE AS THE GENERAL GOALS OF THE MHA CHANGE (see PROCEDURE FOR CHOOSING THE 'RIGHT' PLAN in the previous chapter)

* Preserve the history of Murfreesboro

* Boost the community interest and civic pride

* Improve business along Main St.

🖐 _____
_____
_____
_____
_____

qualities/importance of area

🖐 ADD & DELETE AS THE QUALITIES OF THE AREA CHANGE

The town of Murfreesboro has:

–buildings which exhibit a wide range of architectural examples—including the Federal, Greek Revival, Victorian and Contemporary styles, major works of real architectural distinction (David Barnes house, Myrick house, Uriah Vaughan house) and unusual decoration (Gingerbread house).

–buildings which have a wide range of surface qualities—including color (red, white, yellow), texture (brick, clapboard, board and batten), and shape (Victorian).

Vinson house detail

—a number of interesting single forms—including utilitarian objects (lamps), decorative objects (spider windows), and curiosities (gates).

Gate on Union St.

—buildings with a wide range of architectural relationships—including street facade sequences (south side of W. Main St.; Peter Williams—Murfree Law Office; CBD), and boundaries (fences).

—a wide variety of land and plant forms—topographic features (ravines; Meherrin River), styles of planting design (David Barnes yard; on Union St. south of Vance St. and north of High St.), groups of trees (the two ravines within the historic district; along the river; the ravine between First St. and Moore St.; at David Barnes house; Melrose), unusual

plants (in ravines, especially huge pines in west ravine).

–a large number of viewpoints and landmarks—including forms which dominate or symbolize (the water tower, Uriah Vaughan house, Roberts-Vaughan house), pleasant scenes (Williams St. extension; area directly west of the Wheeler house), panoramic views (corner of Wynn St. and Darlene St.; U.S. 258 bridge

Meherrin River—looking west from U. S. 258 bridge

over Meherrin River), and long vistas (Broad St.; central Main St. and W. Main St.; Vance St.).

–different kinds of urban open spaces—including informal recreation areas (west ravine), parks and public spaces (Riverside Park, Roberts-Vaughan house, High St. Middle School), cemeteries (Thompson, Southall, Wise's), intersections (Williams St. and Main

Southall Cemetery (Hertford Academy in background)

St., Broad St. and Fourth St.), and alleys and backways (driveway between Hertford Academy and Southall cemetery).

–several sites of historic significance—including sites associated with major personalities (Indian Queen Tavern—Lafayette was entertained here in 1825; Walter Reed home—he lived here with his father), sites of single important events (campground and fairground—where a Confederate bivouac was located from 1861 to 1865), and sites of recurring events (Wesleyan Female Institute, Chowan College, Lassiter Hotel, Murfree Law Office).

–a number of social activity sites—including sites of recurring activities (Old Masonic Hall, Hertford Academy) and sites associated with major groups (Roberts-Vaughan—MHA, First Baptist Church).

–a range of visual communication types—including verbal messages (sign in front of Roberts-Vaughan house) and conventional

Roberts–Vaughan house

symbols (barber's sign on Williams St. extension).

🖐 _____
_____
_____

_____
_____
_____
_____
_____
_____
_____
_____
_____
_____
_____
_____
_____

choosing the `right' plan

🖐 EVERYTIME IMPLEMENTATION OF ANY GENERAL OR SPECIFIC SUGGESTION IS CONSIDERED UNDER ANY OF THE FOLLOWING ALTERNATIVE PLANS, GO THROUGH PROCEDURE FOR CHOOSING THE 'RIGHT' PLAN IN THE PREVIOUS CHAPTER

implementing the `right' plan

🖐 IF THE MHA HAS DIFFERENT, BETTER, OR MORE EXACT SUGGESTIONS FOR IMPLEMENTING ANY OF THE FOLLOWING ALTERNATIVE PLANS, GO THROUGH THE DESIGN GUIDELINES IN THE FOLLOWING CHAPTER TO DETERMINE IF THE SUGGESTIONS ARE ACCEPTABLE

Figure 6-3: A page from the Murfreesboro Historic Association workbook, showing the application of qualities, goals, and planning strategies. (Henry Sanoff, _Designing with Community Participation_, Van Nostrand Reinhold, 1978).

SPACE PLANNING

Involving user groups in space planning permits a direct transfer of their knowledge and experience to future design decisions. This involvement also sensitizes participants to the complexities and conflicts inherent in the process.

User space planning was employed in the remodeling of an arts center housed in a vacated city hall building (Sanoff, 1988). After five years of occupancy, funds were secured to make the spatial modifications that would suit the work flow of the organization. In a preliminary study of users' satisfaction with their present environment, often referred to as a postoccupancy evaluation (Wener, 1989), a survey was conducted of arts center staff, members of affiliate organizations, and independent artists who rented studios. Staff members were asked to record their activities, the adequacy of the places where they were performed, the organization of information flow, and the nature of the social environment. The results of the study showed that many of the workspaces were described as being too small and inconveniently located, while the social environment was described as friendly and cooperative. Environmental conditions related to light, temperature, and ventilation contributed to people's satisfaction with their job. Places that were too warm or poorly ventilated were reported to have a direct impact on job performance and satisfaction. Since the building occupants had identified many serious malfunctions in their working environment, a procedure was developed by the design team to permit the users to study the reallocation possibilities of their workplace.

In redesigning the building, participants used graphic symbols corresponding to each activity in the facility to allocate and distribute activities and circulation throughout the building. Each symbol diagram was equivalent to a unit of area. Using floor plans of the existing three-story building, participants used the survey results to establish floor area requirements for all the workspaces. Participants worked in small groups and proposed conflicting solutions which were compared and evaluated to reach a solution that would reconcile their differences.

This approach permitted the building occupants to share their experiences and space concerns with each other as they manipulated the graphic symbols (Figure 6-4a). When each group reached an acceptable solution, the symbols were pasted to the floor plans. The results from all groups were summarized as shown on Figure 6-4b.

The entire staff then reviewed each group's proposal, and modifications were made to the selected best alternative. Finally, a layout was prepared by the design team that satisfied the space and adjacency

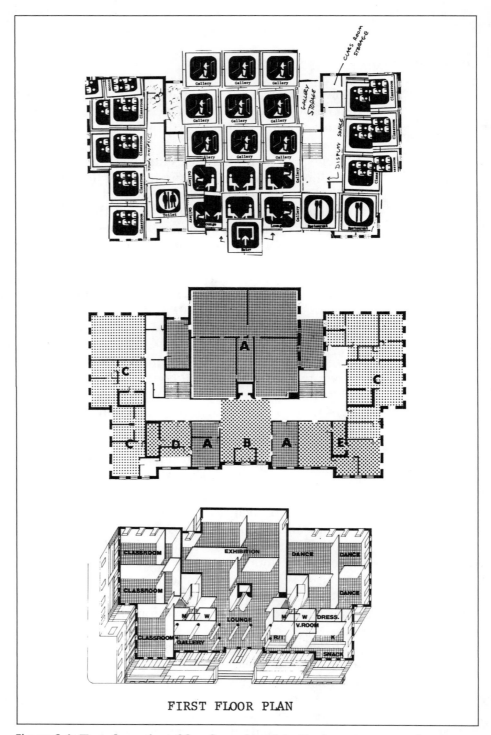

FIRST FLOOR PLAN

Figure 6-4: Transformation of first floor plan of the Durham arts center: A, Galleries; B, Lounge; C, Classrooms; D, Toilets; E, Restaurant (Drawing: Sergio Ortiz & Chainarong Ratanacharoensiri).

requirements for the new facility (Figure 6-4c). The proposed solution was accepted as a natural evolution of the designer/user interaction and not as the designer's ideas that needed to be accepted or rejected.

HOUSING TRADE-OFFS

The concept of *trade-off* is integral to the participatory process, comparing competitive alternatives, particularly according to types of amenities offered. Community groups are often confronted with choices that must be weighed for their appropriateness, since there are often constraints that limit the range of choices. People involved in making trade-offs can evaluate the costs and benefits of available options.

This technique was successfully used in the Durham Owner-Built Housing Process. Ten relatively low income families, who agreed to utilize personal labor as a form of equity in reducing dwelling cost, were identified by a local neighborhood housing service agency. Construction cost was the major constraint within which future home owners would be required to make choices.

While construction cost is always an important consideration, there are also certain family attitudes that are influential in making planning decisions (Sanoff, 1974). Often, people who are confronting a purchase decision look to market choices for a suitable selection rather than examining their work flow and living patterns. Concepts such as family solidarity may influence living patterns and residential preferences in different ways (Jensen, 1952). The opportunity to confront the complexities of spatial interaction, conflicting goals, and privacy needs between members of a family prior to purchase can have a dramatic effect on the selection of a suitable choice.

In order to make the decision process "transparent" in reflecting the value differences among the families, workshops were organized in which decisions about the house were divided into categories of activities, house image, and site arrangements. Faced with budget limitations that influenced the size of the dwelling and the level of amenities, families were able to use the housing trade-off exercise as a preliminary step in discovering their particular residential needs.

The trade-off concept was introduced in the first planning workshop by subdividing the dwelling into activity components such as living–dining and kitchen, or living and dining and kitchen. Three options were provided for the living–eating component of the dwelling, each requiring a different amount of area, signified by the number in the left corner of the picture (Figure 6-5). Similar components were developed for the adults' and children's sleeping areas. Each

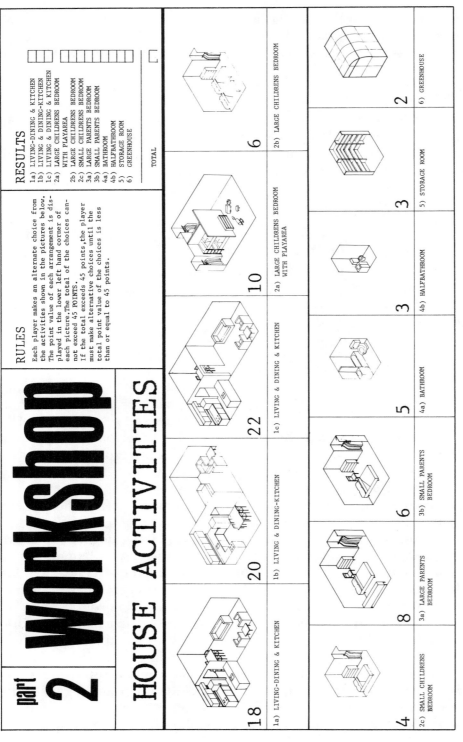

Figure 6-5: Household activity game with assigned points allocated to layout options (Drawing: Alice Brunner, Sergio Ortiz, & Henry Sanoff).

workshop

HOUSE IMAGES

RULES

Each player selects the picture,that he likes the most and that one he dislikes the most.Then he describes the particular charakteristics of the first as well of the last choice.

After each player has completed this step in the process,the individual selections are pooled.Through negotiation the group must agree on the pictures,they like and dislike the most.

PERSONAL RESULTS

like the most: _____

dislike the most: _____

comments: _____ _____ _____

GROUP RESULTS

like the most: _____

dislike the most: _____

comments: _____ _____ _____

Figure 6-6: House images exercise (Photos: Sergio Ortiz & Alice Brunner).

173

family was given an allotment of 45 points which corresponded to their budget and reflected the total area of the dwelling. All family members worked through the process in family groups, making trade-offs between spatial alternatives that provided more or less space for personal or family activities.

The house image exercise considered a series of dwelling photographs that describe subtle and profound character differences (Figure 6-6). This exercise is important in suggesting the ways that buildings convey cues about the values of the people who own and occupy them (Becker, 1977). This environmental message reflecting the inner life, actions, and social conceptions of the occupants (Rapoport, 1982) should be consciously recognized by future home owners. In Housing Image, individuals in small groups make personal choices and discuss their decisions within the group. The process allows families to learn about each others' values, and become aware of the meaning conveyed by different buildings.

The Site Alternatives session allows participants to describe preferences for a variety of site planning characteristics. Through the use of drawings, different rsidential arrangements are depicted that show variations in the amount and type of open space, the location of parking, and the density of the site. While it is improbable that one particular site plan will satisfy all of the participants' requirements, responses suggest the type of site arrangements that meet individual needs. Once participants became familiar with the drawings, the best solutions were chosen for outdoor children's play, privacy, neighborhood activities, and physical security. Individual selections were pooled within small groups for discussion and consensus.

An alternative approach for exploring site options with users is the use of photographs that convey different densities by house type, such as high- and low-rise buildings. The choice of photographic images, whether new or old and single- or multi-family, also suggests the character and location of residential areas, such as inner-city or suburban.

GOAL SETTING IN EDUCATION

A private elementary school chose a participatory planning process to establish better communications between the parents and the teaching staff in developing a long-range building program. The school's building committee invited parents, teachers, and children to become involved in intensive work sessions to collaboratively define their educational goals. Their building plan included a new facility for a proposed kindergarten through twelfth-grade program.

The planning team led by Sanoff (Sanoff and Barbour, 1974)

involved the students by providing them with an opportunity to generate ideas about the school they would like to have. The session opened with the construction of a collaborative poem, a group of statements composed of responses to the phrase, "I wish my school . . ." This approach permitted the students to fantasize about their dream school through an open yet structured process. The results of the wish poem indicated concerns about the administration, curriculum, and the physical environment. A follow-up exercise asked the students to draw pictures of typical and ideal schools based on their mental images. The drawings of the schools conveyed both positive and negative characteristics (Figure 6-7). For example, all the drawings depicted a typical school as a factory-like brick building, similar to the American

Figure 6-7: Children's drawings of a typical school in Africa, in Japan, and in America, as well as their dream school (Henry Sanoff).

stereotype. Their drawings of the ideal school, on the other hand, conveyed a different attitude about a school building and its context: one in which buildings were more complex, angular, and cast in a wooded setting. Other exercises included role-play, where the students assumed adult roles in order to experience the decision-making process in which the building committee, the teachers, and the parents were involved.

A summary of the results of the student exercises constituted the opening of the adult sessions, which set a positive tone for the event. Parents and teachers were sensitized to the importance of the building's image, even to children as young as eleven. The planning team and school community members agreed that a goal-setting process was necessary to develop a basis for a building program. Therefore, as a next step, parents and teachers linked educational objectives, teaching methods, and the physical settings in which they would occur.

Relating Objectives for Learning to Education (ROLE) was the group discussion process developed to familiarize participants with alternative learning methods and places, in which they could contribute their ideas, learn from each other, and learn about planning and design concepts. Similar to a parlor game like Monopoly, rules were developed to permit participants to make individual and group decisions. Beginning with a prepared list of objectives drawn from the educational literature, participants examined how objectives could generate different ways in which learning could occur. For each goal selected, the working groups had to identify four compatible learning methods. For each method chosen, a corresponding student–teacher interaction strategy was chosen. The final step consisted of matching each learning method to a photograph that most closely represented the spatial requirements of the method (Figure 6-8).

ROLE presented the school community members with a technique for assessing the appropriateness of learning places in a school building. Each participant in the process had been given an opportunity to define and defend his or her own ideas and to seek agreement and shared understanding within the group. The five groups participating in the planning sessions selected a total of ten different goals, two of which were common to four of the groups. The final session consisted of amending the statements and establishing priorities for the final list of thirteen objectives.

From this consensual base, an approach was developed for translating the school community's objectives into a framework for developing a building program. The process prevented the "fixing" of concepts too early in the planning stages, by allowing solutions to evolve through discussions of objectives rather than through arguments based

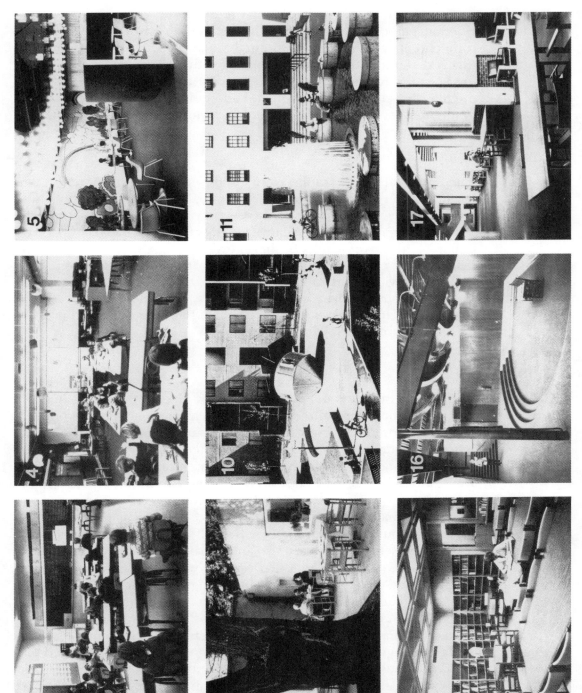

Figure 6-8: Photographs of various school settings (Reprinted from Henry Sanoff, *Design Games*, William Kaufmann, 1979).

on prejudgment. Photographs of the different learning places provided an important link to verbally oriented descriptions of the environment. The building program that developed consisted of data sheets describing the primary learning activity, such as language arts, the learning methods that would support the educational objectives, the teacher–child relationship, and additional information pertaining to the number of students, space requirements, and spatial character.

First Ward School

The identical photographs were used with students, parents, and teachers at First Ward School in Charlotte, North Carolina, who chose a collaborative design process for the expansion of their school. The design team of Morgan Adams asked students to make up "wish poems" and draw pictures of their ideal school. A meeting with thirty teachers and community leaders, working in small groups, listed goals and the activities that supported each goal. Next, they chose settings on the campus for the proposed activities. The photos were fastened to the site plan to indicate where teachers felt their proposed activites fit best (Figure 6-9).

Design in Action

Parents and teachers of the Mary Phillips Magnet School in Raleigh, North Carolina, recognized the need to enrich their school's outdoor play area. Located in a low to middle income black neighborhood, the school provided not only a model integrated educational environment with an outstanding staff and curriculum, but extended day activities for children whose parents worked during the hours of the school's operation from 7 A.M. to 6 P.M. This schedule necessitated more outdoor time than in the typical school, and more than Mary Phillips's basketball court, ballfield, and commercially acquired equipment could serve. The school requested assistance from the Community Design Group (CDG) at the School of Design, North Carolina State University, who had developed a community design approach for incorporating users' ideas during its several years in designing playgrounds (Sanoff, 1982).

In an initial core group meeting selected staff, parents, teachers, and the design team agreed on the importance of a well-designed play area, challenging to children's learning experience. Outdoor activities were seen as a necessary means of releasing energy, providing social interaction, promoting muscle development, and building confidence, as well as reinforcing formal classroom learning. The idea of a com-

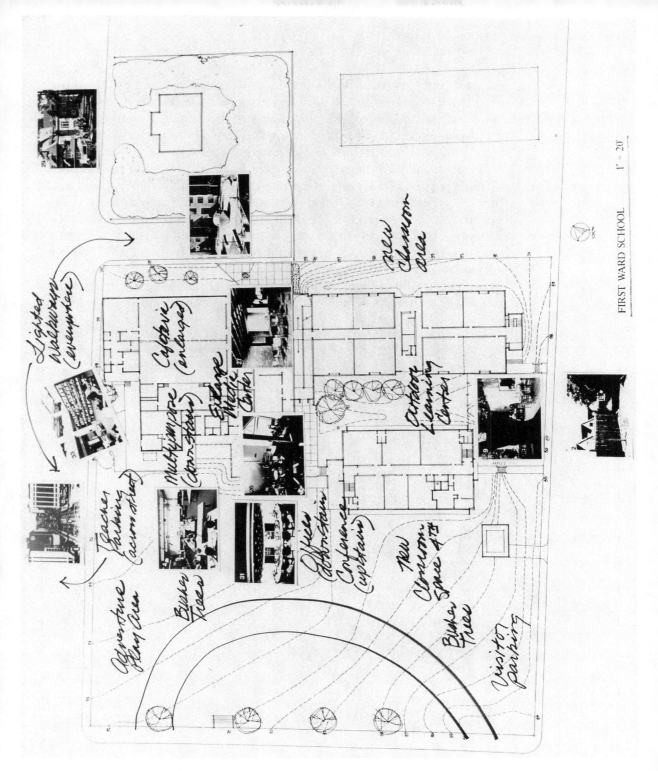

Figure 6-9: Setting photographs used by parents and teachers in the renovation of the First Ward School in Charlotte, North Carolina (Photo: Graham Adams).

munity-built playground was introduced, taking advantage of volunteer effort, donated materials, and local creativity in producing a play area which would reflect the personality of the school. Group members were urged to visit area playgrounds to discover what groups of enthusiastic parents and teachers could achieve.

The next meeting began with a spontaneous discussion of the playgrounds visited. Parents and teachers shared their perceptions and their likes and dislikes. Of the two areas available for playground development, the group chose to concentrate first on the one nearest the classroom building, and then re-examine the other area for supplemental improvements. In beginning to design the area, each participant selected four learning and developmental objectives from the Planning Outdoor Play (POP) game list, then matched each to activities that would fulfill the objectives. Working in groups, members lobbied

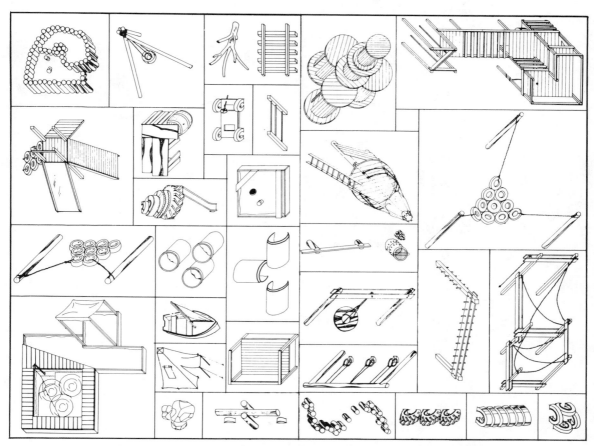

Figure 6-10: Equipment choices for playground planning (Henry Sanoff).

for their individual choices until consensual agreement was reached; the groups then chose representative pieces of equipment appropriate for each activity (Figure 6-10). Finally, groups organized activities and equipment into play zones ranging from passive to active and private to group-natured.

In the Handmade Equipment Layout Planning (HELP) game, the groups related their equipment and zone choices to the play site at the Mary Phillips School. In a parallel exercise, the children's ideas were collected by asking them to design their ideal play area; they drew pictures of most-wanted equipment and described favorite activities. The design team then incorporated ideas generated in all of the exercises into two possible site plans, which integrated new with existing equipment. After discussing both plans with the parent–teacher group, a final plan was prepared.

With the proceeds from a benefit music concert and donations of parents' time, skills, and materials, the new playground was completed in time for the start of the following school year.

CAMPSITE DESIGN

The Pines of North Carolina Council, a regional Girl Scout organization, operates seven campsites in a twenty-county area. Management for the campsites is largely within the volunteer structure of the organization. Although involving council members in decision making is a long-standing tradition in Girl Scouting, it had never occurred in the planning of a campsite. Technical decisions were usually relegated to professional landscape architects, yet growing dissatisfaction with the results of those decisions steered the council to a process involving their own experts in planning, management, and administration. The existing committee system, which included field directors as well as people from public relations, program development, property management, and financial management, was used to form a site development committee. This working committee was responsible for developing campsite proposals with the guidance of NCSU's Community Development Group (Sanoff, Adams, Brasaunas, & Hawkins, 1977).

Campsite Planning

The Pines of Carolina Council had purchased 800 acres as the setting for its new campsite. The site ranged from pine-covered sandhills to environmentally sensitive marshland. The diversity of vegetation, slope, and wildlife habitation presented a variety of environmental settings. Bordering three sides of the site were 50,000 acres of property managed by the North Carolina Wildlife Commission. The executive council appointed a task group to explore developmental alternatives for the campsite and recommend to the Council at large a design proposal for implementation.

The site development committee was asked to investigate conceptual alternatives for a new campsite. The council committee was composed of a diverse group of individuals with expertise in programming, land planning, administration, and facility management. It was apparent that this accumulated knowledge should be constructively integrated into the planning process. To aid in the decision-making process, the Community Development Group was invited to participate as a member of the committee.

Strategy for Outdoor Activity Planning (SOAP) was developed to ensure that there would be a variety of alternatives for campsite development, corresponding with different priorities with the council as well as with the interests of the Girl Scouts themselves. The process was designed to engage people to move collectively through all phases of problem solving—from problem identification to evaluation and decision making.

In order to prepare for collaborative planning, it was necessary for each participant to have visited the site either individually or with a group. Each planning group was given a site plan and a set of photographs depicting the different types of site characteristics. The campsite was analyzed by the design team to provide committee members with information about the natural environment and the ecological systems existing within the site. Interviews were conducted with council staff and field directors about the current programs and future program development. The information generated at this initial stage provided a basic reference for committee members in future decision making. Unique site features included an old cabin occupied by a council ranger, a beaver pond, and a variety of vegetation that related to topographic changes from sandhill to marshland environments. In addition, the site contained a large open field and a six-acre lake.

Results from the site investigation suggested certain guidelines for the development of the campsite, including the need to rebuild an existing dam, reclaim the lake for waterfront activity to expand water resources, and utilize North Carolina Wildlife Commission land for program expansion. Council priorities for new campsite development included enhanced environmental awareness through exploration and expanded potential for educational programs, especially for those not offered at other campsites. Their concerns related to the expressed need for increasing camping skills and self-sufficiency.

Design workshops were the settings in which participants discussed these issues, sharing their common purpose of planning the campsite. Participating Girl Scouts, their parents, council members, and resource people learned from each other as they worked toward decisions.

The workshops began with the construction of a collaborative poem identifying the goals and aspirations of the participants. The poem consisted of completing the phrase, "I wish . . . ," an approach developed to minimize the effort usually expended in stating and defining objectives. The participants' statements were then combined to represent the group's expression of their desires. The results of the wish poem were influential in formulating environmental objectives, the next step in the process.

Similar exercises were conducted with Girl Scout troops in order to provide the planning committee with constructive feedback about the scouts' feelings and their needs regarding campsite development. The wish list represented a combined effort of a number of Girl Scout troops. Although the responses from the scouts varied, important ideas emerged from this effort, such as the desire for year-round camping, evening programs, primitive camping, preservation of wildlife, and tent camping.

A list of environmental objectives for the campsite was then provided to the work groups as an initial point of discussion. Although the objectives were gathered from the Girl Scout literature and the results of the wish poems, the list was not inclusive and was expanded by some groups. While all the objectives seemed desirable, it was helpful for participants to understand different points of view regarding their importance, and to realize that not all were attainable. For effective participation, the committee members were divided into task groups of three to five persons. Group members, most unknown to others, reviewed the environmental objectives list, selected five statements each, and subsequently concurred on those most important. Players were urged to forcefully support their individual choices, even if overlooked by other members of the group. Four outdoor activities were then matched with each objective. When consensus was reached on the selection of appropriate activities, they were located on the campsite plan (Figure 6-11). Each participant was sufficiently familiar with the site so that locational choices corresponded to the appropriate terrain conditions. Locational decisions were made by positioning symbols representing each activity on the site plan. Since the symbols were easily manipulated, it was possible to continuously explore locational alternatives. The site plan simulated the campsite conditions, and the six photographs, located adjacent to the plan, characterized the most

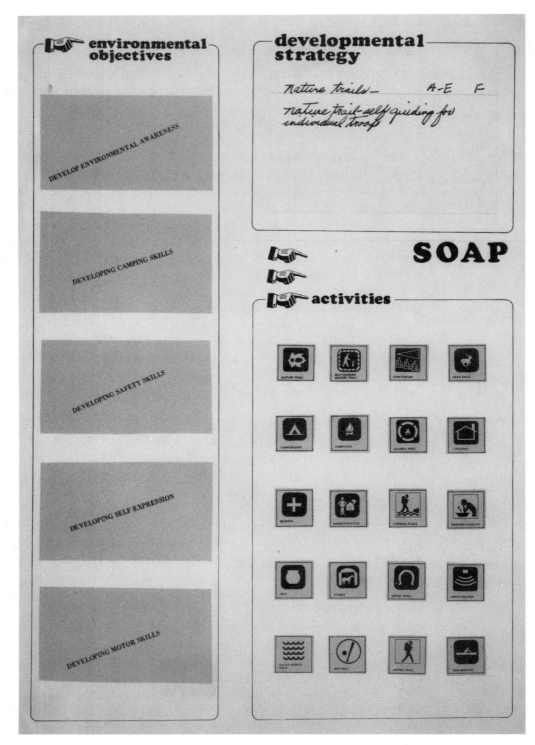

Figure 6-11: Campsite gameboard illustrating environmental objectives, activities and the site plan showing activity choices made by workshop participants (Henry Sanoff & Graham Adams).

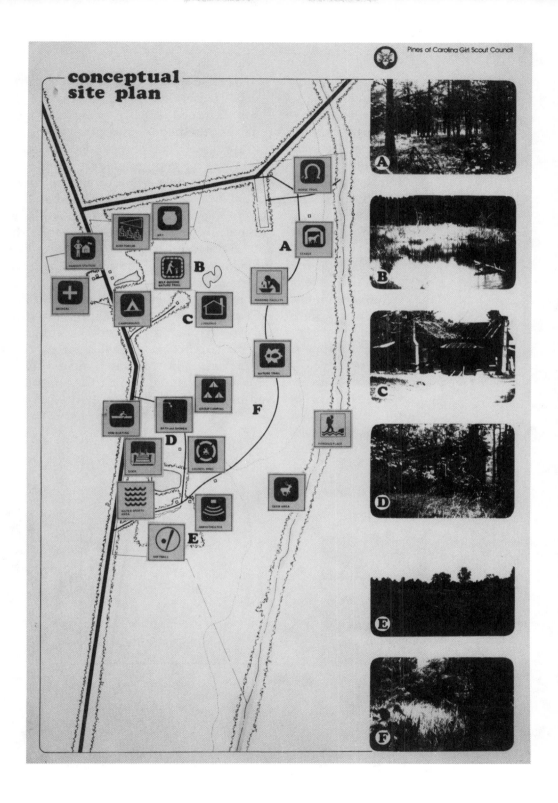

conceptual site plan

Pines of Carolina Girl Scout Council

important site features. Objective and activity cards were pasted by participants on large sheets of paper adjacent to the plan of the campsite. The symbols were then fastened directly onto the preferred site location once the group had reached consensus. A member from each group then presented and discussed its results in order to identify the major points of both conflict and agreement among groups.

There was an agreement on minimum development of the site with an emphasis on environmental preservation. A detailed analysis of the site indicated that any development of the northern portion of the site would seriously harm the natural ecological systems, while the southern area could accommodate the intense activity proposed. Conflicting ideas included the location for tent camping, types of lakefront activities, and the inclusion of horseback-riding trails.

When agreement was achieved, a site plan and a phased implementation scheme were developed by the design team. Described by the council as a long-range property plan, its purpose was to identify and locate a number of interrelated program facilities that the council wanted to develop and operate. The proposed plan suggested the initial development of the tent camping area in the southern part of the site, renovation of all buildings, the trail system location, and an outdoor amphitheater.

a

b

A similar process was used for the design of a nature trail which incorporated a wide variety of special places that contributed to the sensory development and awareness of its users. Since exploration and discovery complement experience in a nature trail, a procedure was developed to plan the sequential arrangement, occurrence, and frequency of visual elements encountered during the walk (Figure 6-12).

c

e

d

Figure 6-12: Sites features included in the trail design. (a) Exposure; (b) Incident; (c) Change of slope; (d) Change of level; (e) Undulation (Drawings by Henry Sanoff, Graham Adams, & Teresa Hawkins).

In group discovery walks with committee members through the proposed site, certain distinctive physical features were identified, such as change of scale or change of level. These features or visual elements were coded with symbols and sketches; using an enlarged site map, work groups located the symbols adjacent to the physical features they discovered on the exploratory walk. The drawings served as a reference or design guideline for creating the desired environmental experience.

Camp Mu-Sha-Ni, as the new campsite was named, carefully and systematically followed the implementation guidelines established by the site development committee. The initial proposal for developing tent camping in the southern part of the site has already been completed. Two tobacco barns have been converted for troop camping, with an outdoor latrine and fire circle. Additional sleeping shelters have also been constructed in the southern area.

Next, the Pines of Carolina proposes to establish the nature trails, restore the historic cabin as a nature/craft center, and construct an all-year-round camping building. All of these activities were consistent with their larger goal of maintaining the campsite as a natural area for troop and family camping.

Nature Trail

The campsite also provides a varied environment in which to locate a nature trail. The wide range of environmental areas includes lowland pine and hardwood communities, a beaver pond, a creek, and features such as a family cemetery and an abandoned horse stable. The trail design consisted of the physical components, sequential arrangement, and activities. The physical components are the visual elements that shape the trail, such as exposure (Figure 6-12a), incident (Figure 6-12b), change of slope (Figure 6-12c), change in level (Figure 6-12d), or undulation (Figure 6-12e). Once the trail components are identified, the sequential trail layout is designed. The occurrence and frequency of the visual elements will directly effect the overall design of the nature trail. The sequential plan, then, identifies when and where a visual element should occur along the trail. Graphic symbols representing the visual elements are located on the plan of the nature trail (Figure 6-13).

(Facing page)
Figure 6-13: Site plan locating site features with graphic symbols.

MORPHOLOGICAL METHOD: CONTINUING CARE CENTER

Morphological charts are a means of forcing the association of required functions in a facility in order to stimulate ideas for unusual design concepts. The charts encourage divergent thinking and safeguard against overlooking novel solutions to a design problem (Jones, 1970). The procedure requires the use of matrix analysis, in which a list of functions for a continuing care center, such as small and large group dining, lounge, residential, administration, and physical therapy, are used to generate methods for accomplishing the functions, or "options." Several methods should be determined for performing the major functions. Each grid cell of the matrix, then, is considered to be a potential design concept for that function, and its feasibility is

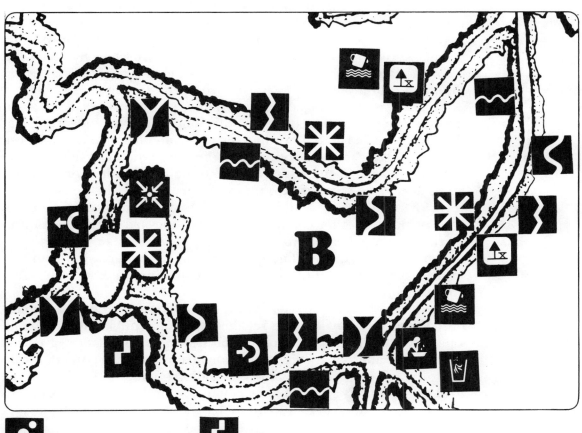

CHANGE OF SCALE

CHANGE OF SLOPE

CHANGE IN LEVEL

UNDULATION

RECESSION-PROJECTION

assessed. The solutions to each cell are selected and connected by a zig-zag line (Figure 6-14), providing a visual display of design options for specific functions.

Diagrams describing spatial options were generated by designers to show variations for each of the primary functions of a continuing care center for the elderly. Figure 6-14 also indicates alternative solutions for some of the functions. Information about appropriate options was gathered from personal observations, interviews, and a review of the geriatric literature. Although the morphological charts that were produced display a number of possible solutions, judgments about the best solution were made through discussions with elderly residents of the community in which the facility was proposed. Five distinct groups with different recreation, housing, health-related needs, and physical limitations were identified. The senior citizens' groups were characterized by their physical condition and self-sufficiency. Those people who were essentially independent were contrasted with people characterized by severe physical and mental limitations, who were not self-sufficient. Arriving at the best solution was accomplished by analyzing rows independently and then connecting the row solutions vertically to form a column solution characterized by the zig-zag line.

An analysis of the objectives for dining, which was regarded as an important activity aside from its nutritional purpose, suggested that this area afforded an opportunity for social interaction and relaxation. Decisions about the best option for large group dining resulted in the selection of one spatial setting for the three independent groups, but it was also agreed that groups four and five, people who needed some form of health care, would require different spatial arrangements. Observations of other continuing care facilities led to the decision to provide a place adjacent to the dining area where people could comfortably wait. A premeal lineup outside the dining area was common in many centers, creating problems by extending into adjacent areas and disrupting activities.

Another use of the morphological method is shown by the numerous design solutions for the rehabilitation of a public housing unit. Energy control strategies, such as solar heating or ventilation, are used to generate alternative design solutions based on environmental control principles, such as blocking or shielding (Figure 6-15). Each of the grid cells contains a functional solution. From this visual display, it is possible to combine design solutions based on preferred strategies and principles.

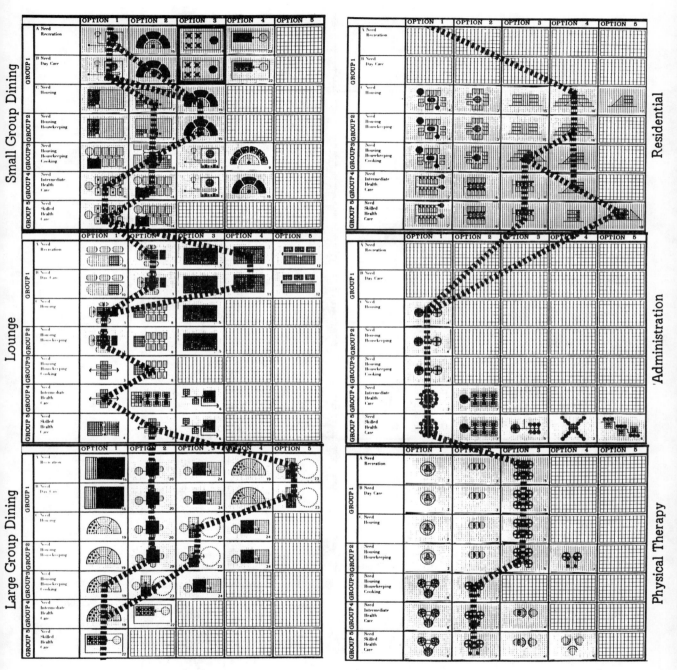

Figure 6-14: Morphological chart for continuing care center, showing patterns of solutions (Drawing: Joel Chou & Henry Sanoff).

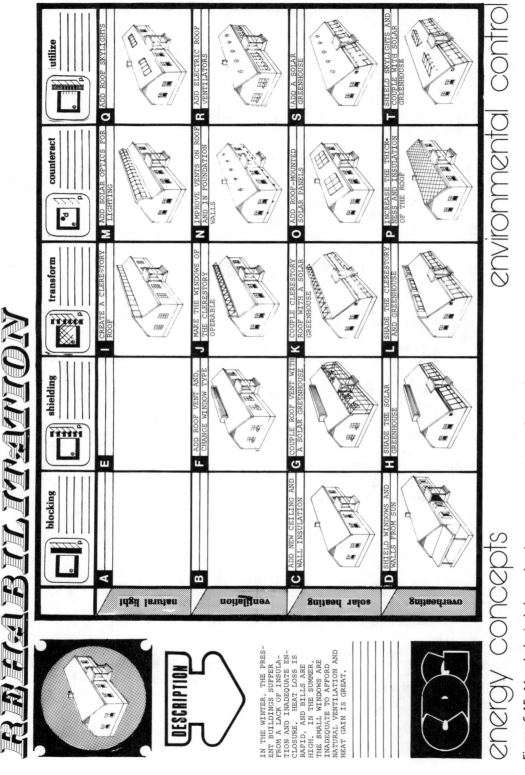

Figure 6-15: Morphological charts showing energy concepts and control measures for housing rehabilitation (Drawing: Joel Chou & Henry Sanoff).

PLANNING BALLOT

The Yerba Buena Center Renewal Project has been the focus of more than twenty years of planning, dissention, controversy, and litigation. In one year alone, more than five different alternative plans for developing YBC were proposed. In turn, these plans have been the subject of more controversy, numerous meetings, committees, speeches, press releases, and debates, all of which tended to raise the level of public information and interest without providing any effective way for people to register opinions, make decisions, or select from the potpourri of plans and proposals. The situation had the effect of giving more importance to the views of a few protagonists than to those of ordinary citizens.

The Yerba Buena Planning Ballot (Turner, 1978) was conceived as a way to overcome this situation, to broaden active citizen participation by providing those who do not or cannot attend or speak out at public meetings with a medium for expressing their feelings and ideas. The ballot was designed to provide residents of the south of Market area with a means of expressing their preferences on what should or should not be built in the Yerba Buena Urban Renewal Project. This area of San Francisco was most directly affected by the project, with a large population of low-income minority families and elderly residents whose needs and aspirations received the least consideration, and whose views were not often solicited or otherwise obtained.

The ballot was made up of three parts: three propositions outlining the major alternative plan concepts, thirteen policy statements dealing with the Yerba Buena project area, and a selection of land uses from which people could devise their own plan for YBC (Figure 6-16). The detachable portion could be mailed or placed in one of the YBC ballot boxes located in the south of the Market area.

The Yerba Buena Planning Ballot enabled people to design their own plan for YBC. Together, the three parts of the ballot provided people with a way to organize and express their preferences on the most important facets of a large complex urban renewal project: on overall concepts; on policies; on individual land uses; and on activities allowing interaction of design, policy, and administration. The ballot provided a realistic context for citizens to order their preferences, and served as a tool for planners, designers, and policy makers to measure public relations and preferences on a variety of planning issues.

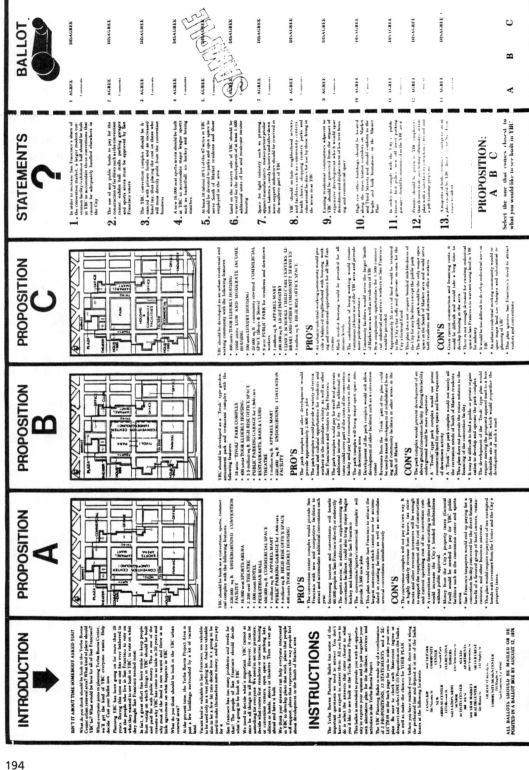

Figure 6-16: Yerba Buena planning ballot (Reprinted from Henry Sanoff, *Designing with Community Participation*, Van Nostrand Reinhold, 1978).

HOUSING ASSEMBLY KIT

In the design of Council housing in central London, architect Nabs Hamdi created a new series of communication aids to encourage user participation in design (Low, 1980). His tools allowed people to take control of organizing their space, faced at the same time with the consequences of their decisions. The project was described as Primary Support System and Housing Assembly Kit (PSSHAK).

Hamdi defined areas of public and private decision making, confirming the architect's role in the public decision-making area—the designing of the shell and the assembly kit of parts of the dwellings—while leaving the tenants free to establish their priorities for the interior of their homes. Hamdi described himself as an "enabler" and "facilitator" as he explained the scheme in a brochure and numerous planning sessions for tenants. A questionnaire simultaneously established whether the family had any particular requirements in terms of living space or room combinations. Tenants had the use of a model to assist them in initial planning of the layout of their dwelling units according to ages and interests and in adapting these arrangements to charges in family circumstances. Specially drawn gridded floors with pin-on furniture were used (Figure 6-17).

Figure 6-17: Model components developed for participants in the PSSHAK process (Photo: Nabeel Hamdi).

The PSSHAK approach rests on the separation of the building structure from internal space-dividing elements. This enables a variety of dwelling sizes and mixes independent of the structure. The number and sizes of rooms can be modified with the use of an adjustable system of internal walls.

The idea of the small housing estate is derived from N. John Habraken's (1972) *Support Structures*. Consisting of a concrete frame several stories high, with horizontal and vertical communication systems, the estate stretches out through the town; complete dwellings were to be slotted in from manufacturers' catalogues and showrooms like books in a bookcase. The dwellings were to be assembled by their future residents.

Adelaide Road Housing estate was the only British application where blocks of dwellings were the support structures and the interior was divided into separate rooms of the dwelling. At Adelaide Road, the level of participation appeared to have been intense, since many of the tenants took the planning seriously.

A housing appraisal kit, developed by the Greater London Council (GLC) in association with the Department of the Environment, was used to assess the residents' satisfaction with the Adelaide Housing Project after occupancy. The appraisal kit is a social survey method for helping local authorities find out what their tenants think about the housing projects designed by GLC. When examining the relationship of participation to satisfaction, it appeared that almost two-thirds of the people who participated in the internal design of their dwelling felt their requirements had been fulfilled. Generally, the residents believed that overall satisfaction could be increased by extending user participation to the external design of the housing estates.

COMMUNITY LIBRARY

Two events in the community life of rural Boulder Creek, California, catalyzed local efforts to plan and construct a new library. The unincorporated village, located in northern Santa Cruz County, eighty miles south of San Francisco and thirteen miles north of the city of Santa Cruz, was unprepared to meet emergency needs during the nationally publicized flooding and mudslides of 1982. Cut off from urban services provided by the city of Santa Cruz, the area lacked badly needed emergency facilities and meeting locations to cope with loss of life and housing. In the wake of the experience, the residents trained themselves in emergency response techniques and reaffirmed the need for a self-sufficient community center and meeting place.

Second, a library site was donated in the downtown Boulder Creek area within walking distance of most of the community. At the time, library services were provided in a small storefront branch library on Highway 9, the village's main street.

With the direction of a county supervisor who was trained as an architect and was an active proponent of citizen participation in design and planning, the County of Santa Cruz released a Request for Proposals for the design of the Boulder Creek Branch Library. The RFP stressed maximum energy efficiency, including use of natural light and passive solar principles, and the inclusion of a community participation process to ensure responsiveness to community needs and desires. The request included program and space requirements identified by a library advisory committee composed of library staff, city and county officials, and appointed citizens, and an additional list of community function spaces. The City/County Library Advisory Committee selected the architectural firms of Van der Ryn/Calthorpe of Sausolito and Jeff Orberdorfer (1989) of Santa Cruz to collaborate on the design. The former were known for their work in energy-conserving design, and the latter for his demonstrated commitment to citizen participation.

Three workshops were planned to elicit ideas from groups, working toward consensus solutions on specific design problems. At the first workshop a general brainstorming session was held to generate a series of concepts for the library and to stimulate discussion. A list of forty-three concepts such as, "The library should be a home away from home and always be open" and "The library should have a large, open entry—inviting to everyone," was compiled. Following a break, participants worked in small groups, graphically illustrating patterns of images of parts of the library to suggest its desired feeling or ambiance.

At the second workshop, a group of people who lived adjacent to the library building site expressed concerns about the effect that the proposed facility would have on the neighborhood; specifically, they anticipated increased noise from arriving cars, parking problems, teenagers "hanging out" in the area, and a general increase in noise and litter. These potential problems were considered along with the established program and suggested concepts and images, as small groups produced floor plans and site plans. Most of the designs included an east-facing entry, using the building to buffer noise from the surrounding neighborhood (Figure 6-18). Conscious of solar factors, most groups located the central reading room to the south, and added outdoor decks to the floor plan. An unexpected event reinforced the community participation intent: a local artist was so excited by the enthusiasm evident in the workshop that she offered to produce a figurative sculpture for the library. Participants encouraged her to

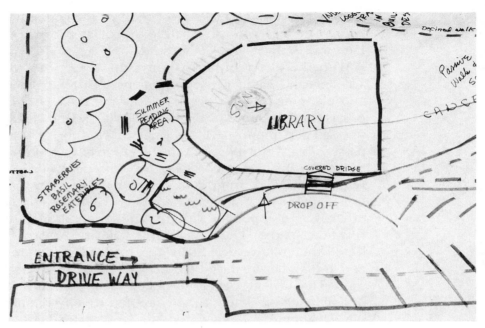

Figure 6-18: Consensus group site plan for the Boulder Creek, California, library (Drawing: Jeff Oberdorfer, Jeff Oberdorfer & Associates, Architects).

bring a model to the next session. After the workshops were completed, other area artists contributed stained glass, ceramic tiles, and other artwork, which were incorporated in the building.

After analyzing the various plans produced at the second workshop, the architects developed a consensus plan and model to present at the third and final workshop. A slide show simulated the building on the site and illustrated how the participants' suggested patterns had been incorporated into the design. To promote faithful implementation, six participants volunteered to continue meeting with the architects and Library Advisory Committee and to schedule representatives to appear in support of the library design at public hearings of the City/County Library Commission and the county board of supervisors.

Citizens successfully carried the interests of the workshop participants through the hearing and approval process. The board of supervisors and library commission unanimously approved the proposed design, and the Boulder Creek Branch Library opened in March 1985 with a major community celebration. Two years later, the library received a national design award from the American Institute of Architects.

WORKING TOGETHER

The task of designing a worship place for a community that holds a wide variety of views about theology, and whose approval of the design must be obtained, offers particular challenge to any architect. After a forest fire destroyed their old A-frame church, members of the Episcopal parish of St. Matthew in the Pacific Palisades section of Los Angeles held a number of opinions about what their new church should be like, including how big it should be, what it should look like, where on the thirty-seven-acre site it should be located, and how it might incorporate the prayer garden that was associated with the earlier building.

In seeking an architect who could propose an appropriate building, the church's building committee ruled that the selected design would have to be approved by a two-thirds positive vote of the 350-member congregation. Architects Charles Moore and partners John Ruble and Buzz Yudell were willing to accept the committee's conditions, and decided that the only way to secure the congregation's approval was to let them design the building (Moore, 1984). With the help of Jim Burns, who with Lawrence Halprin had invented the "Take Part" workshop process, the architects held a series of four Sunday workshops, one each month, during which the design was developed.

The first workshop began with an awareness walk to identify places on the property where the church might be sited. Later in the day, participants were given sample materials—including *Froot Loops*, parsley, and cellophane—with which to make models of the church that they wanted. When the architects returned a month later with more sophisticated model kits of exterior and interior elements (pews, altars, choirs, bell towers, and so on), each of the seven tables of fifteen to twenty parishioners "miraculously" (according to Moore) produced the same plan. Each scheme suggested a half-circle or half-ellipse of pews embracing the altar, putting the congregation in close communication with the service and avoiding views of fellow parishioners beyond. There was varying opinion about an appropriate backdrop; some wished to see the prayer garden behind the altar, while others wished to view the officiators without distraction from the California landscape.

During a slide show of some eighty churches around the world, everyone was encouraged to voice opinions about likes and dislikes, and to suggest appropriate models for the new St. Matthew's. The least popular was St. Peter's in Rome (perhaps for doctrinal as well as architectural reasons), and the most popular was Alvar Aalto's Vuoksenniska Church at Imatra, Finland. The choice of the latter, white masonry building was somewhat surprising given the older parishioners' preference for a wood church like their beloved previous one.

In the third meeting the participants again showed agreement in selecting a roof shape for the building. Of the set of large-scale models presented, five of the six tables of parishioners chose a modified Latin cross with long dormers for transepts (Figure 6-19). The architects were thus presented with the interesting assignment of fitting a Latin-cross roof on a half-elliptical plan. This was achieved, along with adding a chapel, baptistry, ancillary rooms, and an outdoor patio. In the fourth session the group offered detailed suggestions, some almost contradictory. Some wanted a simple church, others a noble, cathedral-like space. The architects' solution was to propose a grand interior nave crowned by two, thirty-six-foot-high arches (to accommodate the new pipe organ) with the cruciform roof superimposed on a broad hip roof with low eaves. The transepts, or dormers, terminated in round rose windows with simple orthogonal mullions like the sash of Bernard Maybeck's Christian Science Church in Berkeley. Courtyards were included to draw in the existing trees.

Figure 6-19: Community review of model options for St. Matthew Church, Pacific Palisades, California (Photo: courtesy of Moore Ruble Yudell).

Among the interior details that required negotiation were the selection of floor and wall surfaces and the character of the reredos behind the altar. Plaster walls, with a pattern of deep wood battens two feet apart, were designed to provide the proper heavy accoustical backdrop for the organ without sacrificing the desired wood interior. After considering several (unpopular) proposals for the reredos (including a blank wall, an "Advent calendar" of saints in niches, and a set of fifteen-foot-high figures of the evangelists), the group accepted the rector's suggestion of a Tree of Life.

In their vote about the design, siting, and details of the new church, 83 percent of the congregation were favorable to the collaborative scheme that the participants and architects had developed. More than two years of design development followed, in which the parishioners continued to participate. The excitement and cooperative spirit generated by the design process carried the project through the necessary financial arrangements among the congregation, and then final construction. St. Matthew's was rewarded not only with a building with which they were pleased, but by the unexpected medieval quality of the sound of their new organ with it.

DESIGN TELETHON

Like many mid-sized cities in America, Roanoke, Virginia, suffered economic and physical decline when suburban shopping malls began to overshadow locally based commerce. The change from steam to electric trains alone severely affected the city's job base, and essentially ended the city's history as the railroad and trade center of the Shenandoah Valley. Outlying development further undercut the former railroad hub, which had been especially hard-hit during the Depression. In the last half-century, residents had internalized the physical isolation created by the surrounding Blue Ridge Mountains. When yet another shopping mall was announced in the mid 1970's, concerted effort was needed if the area was to survive. The city consulted the architects of Centerbrook of Essex, Connecticut, who decided to use television to involve the area in a several-month, design-a-thon, an electronic town meeting in which ideas could be presented and pursued before a limitless audience of active participants.

Late in 1978 architects J. P. Chadwick Floyd and Trip Wyeth literally moved into town, set up shop in a storefront office, and invited people to come by to discuss what was wrong with Roanoke and what could be done to fix it. Conscious of the community consensus that city manager Bern Ewett had insisted was essential, the team met with a fifteen-member steering committee of business and civic leaders and a fifty-member design workshop to get a sense of community ideas and "the lay of the land" (Crosbie, 1984).

The first of four television events in the "Roanoke Design '79" series was held in late September 1978 during prime time on the local CBS affiliate. The redevelopment design team was introduced, and viewers were invited to call in their ideas as the project area, divided into seven districts, was described with brightly colored maps and graphics. As each area was considered, members of the design workshop relayed phone calls to Chadwick Floyd, who discussed ideas on the air. Some proposals, such as the suggestion to use a dome to create a pedestrian retail mall, were pursued instantaneously; as Floyd spoke with the viewer, architect Charles Moore began to sketch the dome, and a financial consultant considered the economic feasibility of the project. Other ideas were recorded on large sheets on the walls. Local business and civic leaders were interviewed about their roles in the redevelopment. At the close of the hour broadcast there was a recap of the ideas collected, and the design team returned to their storefront headquarters to consider each one (Figure 6-20).

During the second show, sketches of development alternatives for the districts were presented. Viewers had in hand copies of the alternatives and a map published in the local newspaper, and callers phoned in their suggestions for changes. Votes for preferences were sent in, and in the following month the plan was refined. In the third show, structures proposed for the final plan were presented in model form. In an unexpected live event, a top executive of Blue Cross Blue Shield announced on the air that the company would locate new offices in downtown Roanoke, just as the architects were discussing the site on which such offices might be located. According to Neilson ratings, the show drew 90,000 viewers.

In the fourth show, aired in January 1979 after continued work by the architects, steering committee, city government, and design workshop, the plan was presented in final form. Each project area was discussed in detail. A total of fifty-nine individual projects was proposed, requiring $47.2 million in private investment and $17.4 million in public investment. Within three years the citizens of Roanoke approved bond issues to fund all but seven of the projects; within five years, $88.9 in private funds, $24.7 million in city funds, and $17.4 million in state and federal funds had been invested.

The city manager attributed the success of the plan to the dynamism of citizen involvement. Because of its development on television, the plan was composed of individual pieces rather than the traditional single, large sweeping scheme. "That's the way cities are supposed to be—made up of a lot of little things," Floyd said. The success of the

Figure 6-20: Cable television planning for Roanoke, Virginia (Photo: Chad Floyd, courtesy of Centerbrook).

plan did not depend on execution of the whole. Further, detailed focus on individual projects allowed the citizens to better grasp and appreciate the ideas proposed. Centerbrook presented its report to the city in a loose-leaf binder catalog, what Floyd described as a "shopping list of ideas," through which any or all of the fifty-nine projects could be pursued. The format allowed the city to remove impractical ideas and to update others.

Before architects were chosen to execute the plan, the individual projects were divided into three categories according to the amount of management that would be required by a design management team, composed of Centerbrook and its joint-venture partners Hayes, Seay, Mattern & Mattern (HSMM) of Roanoke and landscape architect Lester Collins of Millbrook, New York. By stipulating the amount of supervision needed by each project, the management team hoped to maintain an appropriate level of design quality in each project according to its role in the overall plan, to control the budget, and to complete the plan within a time period during which public support could be sustained.

The results of the plan so far are deemed to be highly successful, reflecting both a comfortable human and city scale. The revitalized market district is considered to be the focal point of the city. In an area once characterized by vagrants and adult bookstores, there is now a multi-use cultural center in a rehabilitated warehouse, new stalls for vendors in the farmers' market, a pocket park, and the newly renovated market building housing a retail food center and specialty shops. Market Square now serves as a backdrop for many community festivals. A tree-lined walkway with reflecting pools links the market to new development to the south, including a new parking garage, an IBM office buiding, redesigned Elmwood Park with new street furniture and an open-air performance stage, a new library extension, and the Blue Cross Blue Shield building.

The Roanoke Design '79 campaign has produced other benefits aside from the physical rebirth of the city. Citizens have come to expect to be involved in other city projects. They are more aware of the history and architectural quality of their city and are proud of the unique resources they have to share and enjoy. Residents initiated redevelopment in the sixteen residential neighborhoods, and individual improvement projects have been undertaken by community members who are now sensitive to issues of architecture, scale, and design. In the words of steering committee member E. K. Mattern, "Roanoke underwent a mental revitalization, and it changed attitudes."

References

Acking, Carl-Axel, and Rikard Küller. 1973. Presentation and judgement of planned environment and the hypothesis of arousal. In *Environmental Design Research*, ed. Wolfgang F.E. Preiser, pp. 72–83. Stroudsburg, PA: Dowden, Hutchinson & Ross.

Appleton, Jay. 1975. *The Experience of Landscape*. New York: Wiley.

Appleyard, Donald. 1970. Styles and methods of structuring a city. *Environment and Behavior* 2(1): 100–116.

Appleyard, Donald, Kevin Lynch, and John R. Meyer. 1964. *The View from the Road*. Cambridge: Massachusetts Institute of Technology.

Appleyard, Donald, and Lois Fishman. 1977. High-rise building versus San Francisco: Measuring visual and symbolic impacts. In *Human Responses to Tall Buildings,* ed. Donald J. Conway. pp. 81–100. Stroudsburg, PA: Dowden, Hutchinson & Ross.

Armstrong, Helen, and Craig Burton. 1986. *Street Tree Survey: NSW Country Towns*. University of New South Wales, Department of Landscape Architecture.

Arnheim, Rudolf. 1954. *Art and Visual Perception: A Psychology of the Creative Eye*. Berkeley: University of California Press.

Bachelard, Gaston. 1964. *The Poetics of Space*. New York: Orion Press.

Bechtel, Robert B. 1965. Participation and observation in the mental hospital. *Kansas Journal of Sociology,* 1: 166–74.

Bechtel, Robert B. 1977. *Enclosing Behavior*. Stroudsburg, PA: Dowden Hutchinson & Ross.

Bechtel, Robert B. and John Zeisel. 1987. Observation: The world under glass. In *Methods in Environment and Behavioral Research*, ed. Robert B. Bechtel, Robert W. Marans, and William Michelson, pp. 11–40. New York: Van Nostrand Reinhold.

Beck, Robert, and Denis Wood. 1976. Cognitive transformation of information from urban geographic fields to mental maps. *Environment and Behavior* 8(2): 199–238.

Becker, Franklin. 1977. *Housing Messages*. Stroudsburg, PA: Dowden Hutchinson & Ross.

Bentz, Bruce. 1980. *Transition: User Participation in the Design of Housing,* London: Department of Design Research, Royal College of Art.

Berlyne, Daniel E. 1958. The influence of complexity and novelty in visual figures on orienting responses. *Journal of Experimental Psychology,* 55: 289–296.

Berlyne, Daniel E. 1960. *Conflict, Arousal, and Curiosity.* New York: McGraw Hill.

Berlyne, Daniel E. 1972. Ends and means of experimental aesthetics. *Canadian Journal of Psychology,* 26: 303–325.

Berlyne, Daniel E., and S. Peckham. 1966. The semantic differential and other measures of reaction to visual complexity. *Canadian Journal of Psychology.* 20(2): 125–135.

Bishop, Jeff. 1977. CRIG Analysis. *Bulletin of Environmental Education* 73: 3–8.

Bishop, Jeff, and Graham Russell. 1984. *The Houses Game.* Bristol, England: Resources for Learning Development Unit.

Bishop R. 1983. *The perception and importance of time in architecture.* Ph.D thesis, University of Surrey.

Bonta, Juan Pablo. 1979. Simulation games in architectural education. *Journal of Architectural Education,* 33(1): 154–156.

Boulding, Kenneth E. 1964. *The Image.* Ann Arbor, MI: University of Michigan.

Brunswik, Egon. 1956. *Perception and the Representative Design of Psychological Experiments.* Berkeley: University of California Press.

Burns, Jim. 1979. *Connections: Ways to Discover and Realize Community Potentials.* New York: McGraw Hill.

Canter, David. 1969. An intergroup comparison of connotative dimensions in architecture. *Environment and Behavior,* 1, 37–48.

Canter, David. 1970. Should we treat building users as subjects or objects? In *Architectural Psychology,* ed. David Canter, pp. 11–18. London: RIBA Publication.

Canter, David. 1977. *The Psychology of Place.* London: Architectural Press.

Canter, David. 1983. The purposive evaluation of places: A facet approach. *Environment and Behavior,* 15(6): 659–698.

Canter, David, Jennifer Brown, and Linda Groat. 1985. A multiple sorting procedure for studying conceptual systems. In *The Research Interview: Uses and Approaches,* eds. Michael Brenner, Jennifer Brown, and David Canter, pp. 79–113, London: Academic Press.

Cashden, Lisa, Bernd Fahle, Mark Francis, Steven Schwartz, and Peter Stein. 1978. A critical framework for participatory approaches to environmental change. In *Participatory Planning and Neighborhood Control*, ed. Mark Francis. New York: Center for Human Environments, CUNY.

Chang, Ching-Yu. 1978. Works by Lawrence Halprin. *Process: Architecture*. 4.

Cherem, G. J. 1973. Looking through the eye of the public or public images as social indications of aesthetic opportunity. *In Toward a Technique for Quantifying Aesthetic Quality of Water Resources*, ed. P. J. Brown, PRWG-120-2, pp. 52–64. Utah State University, Institute of Water Resources. Logan.

Collier, John. 1979. Visual anthropology. In *Images of Information*, ed. Jon Wagner, pp. 271–281. Beverly Hills, CA: Sage Publications.

Collier, John. 1986. *Visual Anthropology*. Fort Worth, TX: Holt, Rinehart and Winston.

Conklin, Harold C. 1976. Ethnographic semantic analysis of Ifugao landform categories. In *Environmental Knowing*, eds. Gary T. Moore and Reginald G. Golledge, pp. 235–46. Stroudsburg, PA: Dowden, Hutchinson & Ross.

Cooper, Claire. 1975. *Easter Hill Village: Some Social Implications of Design*. New York: Free Press.

Craik, Kenneth H. 1968. The comprehension of the everyday physical environment. *Journal of the American Institute of Planners*, 34(1): 29–37.

Craik, Kenneth H. 1971. The assessment of places. In *Advances in Psychological Assessment, Vol. 2*, ed. Paul McReynolds, Palo Alto, CA: Science and Behavior Books.

Craik, Kenneth H., and George E. McKechnie. 1974. *Perception of Environmental Quality: Preferential Judgments versus Comparative Appraisals*. Unpublished manuscript. University of California, Berkeley.

Craik, Kenneth H. and Ervin H. Zube. 1976. *Perceiving Environmental Quality: Research and Applications*. New York: Plenum.

Crosbie, Michael. 1984. Television as a tool of urban design. *Architecture*, 73(11): 54–60.

Crosley, Mark L. 1988. *The Architect's Guide to Computer-Aided Design*. New York: Wiley.

Cullen, Gordon. 1971. *The Concise Townscape*. London: Architectural Press.

Daniel, Terry C., and Ron S. Boster. 1976. Measuring landscape aesthetics: The Scenic Beauty Estimation method (Research paper RM-167). Fort Collins, CO: U.S. Department of Agriculture, Rocky Mountain Forest and Range Experiment Station.

Daniel, Terry C., and Joanne Vining. 1983. Methodological issues in the assessment of visual landscape quality. In *Behavior and the Natural Environ-*

ment, eds. Irwin Altman and Joachim Wohlwill, pp. 39–84. New York: Plenum.

Davis, Gerald, and Virginia Ayers. 1975. Photographic recording of environmental behavior. In *Behavioral Research Methods,* ed. William Michelson, pp. 235–79. Stroudsburg, PA: Dowden, Hutchinson & Ross.

Davis, Susan J. 1981. *Close Encounters with the Built Environment.* Canada: Evergreen Press.

Day, Hy. 1965. Attention, curiosity and exploration. In *Design and Planning,* ed. Martin Krampen, pp. 42–48. Waterloo, Ontario: University of Waterloo Press.

Downs, Roger, and David Stea. 1973. Cognitive maps and spatial behavior: Process and products. In *Image and Environment: Cognitive Mapping and Spatial Behavior,* eds. Roger M. Downs and David Stea, pp. 8–26. Chicago: Aldine.

Downs, Roger M., and David Stea. 1977. *Maps in Mind.* New York: Harper & Row.

Dubos, Renes, 1967. Man adapting. In *Environment for Man,* ed. William R. Ewald, Jr., pp. 19–20. Bloomington, IN: Indiana University Press.

Esser, Aristide H., and T. L. Etter. 1966. Automated location recording on a psychiatric ward: Preliminary notes on continuous monitoring of posture and movement of all individuals in an observation area. *American Zoologist,* 6: 251.

Evans, Gary W., David G. Marrero, and Patricia A. Butler. 1981. Environmental learning and cognitive mapping. *Environment and Behavior* 13(1): 83–104.

Farbstein, Jay, and Min Kantrowitz. 1976. *People and Places.* Englewood Cliffs, NJ: Prentice Hall.

Faulkner, H. William. 1985. Simulation games as a technique for information collection: A case study of disabled person transport use in Canberra. In *Survey Interviewing: Theory and Techniques,* ed. Terence W. Breed and Robert J. Stimson, pp. 95–105. Sydney: Allen and Unwin.

Feimer, Nickolaus R. 1984. Environmental perception: The effect of media evaluative context, and the observer sample. *Journal of Environmental Psychology,* 4(1): 61–80.

Festinger, Lionel. 1964. *Conflict, Decision, and Dissonance.* London: Tavistock.

Foley, James D. 1987. Interfaces for advanced computing. *Scientific American,* 256(4): 126–35.

Francis, Mark. 1988. Negotiating between children and adult design values in open space projects. *Design Studies,* 9(2): 67–75.

Freid, Marc, and Peggy Gleicher. 1961. Some sources of residential satisfaction in an urban slum. *Journal of the American Institute of Planners*, 29: 179–198.

Friedman, Arnold, Craig Zimring, and Ervin Zube. 1978. *Environmental Design Evaluation*. New York: Plenum.

Gärling, Tommy, Anders Book, and Erik Lindberg. 1986. Spatial orientation and wayfinding in the designed environment: A conceptual analysis and some suggestions for post-occupancy evaluation. *Journal of Architectural and Planning Research*, 3(1): 55–64.

Gärling, Tommy, and Reginald G. Golledge. 1989. Environmental perception and cognition. In *Advances in Environment, Behavior and Design, Volume 2,* eds. Ervin H. Zube and Gary T. Moore, pp. 203–30. New York: Plenum.

Gehl, Jan. 1987. *Life Between Buildings: Using Public Spaces*. New York: Van Nostrand Reinhold.

Gibson, James J. 1971. The information available in pictures. *Leonardo* 4: 27–35.

Gibson, James J. 1979. *The Ecological Approach to Visual Perception*. Boston: Houghton Mifflin.

Golledge, Reginald G. 1976. Methods and methodological issues in environmental cognition research. In *Environmental Knowing,* eds. Gary T. Moore and Reginald G. Golledge, pp. 300–14. Stroudsburg, PA: Dowden, Hutchinson & Ross.

Golledge, Reginald G. 1987. Environmental cognition. In *Handbook of Environmental Psychology,* eds. Dan Stokols and Irving Altman, New York: Wiley.

Goodey, Brian. 1974. *Images of Place: Essays on Environmental Perception, Communication, and Education.* Center for Urban & Regional Studies, University of Birmingham.

Goodey, Brian. 1974. *Urban Walks and Town Trails.* Centre for Urban and Regional Studies. University of Birmingham.

Goodey, Brian. 1977. Sensing the environment. *Bulletin of Environmental Education.* 72: 3–10.

Gould, Peter R., and Rodney White. 1974. *Mental Maps*. Hammondsworth, England: Penguin.

Grainger, B. 1980. *A study of concepts in the building design process*. MSc. dissertation, University of Surrey.

Greenbie, Barrie B. 1976. *Design for Diversity*. New York: Elsevier.

Gregson, Robert A.M. 1964. Aspects of the theoretical status of aesthetic response typologies. *Psychology Reports*, 5(10): 395–398.

Grey, Arthur L., Gary H. Winkel, David L. Bonsteel, and Roger A. Parker. 1970. *People and Downtown: Use, Attitudes, and Settings.* Seattle: University of Washington, College of Architecture and Urban Planning.

Groat, Linda N. 1981. Meaning in architecture: New directions and sources. *Journal of Environmental Psychology,* 1(1): 73–85.

Groat, Linda N. 1982. Meaning in post-modern architecture: An examination using the multiple sorting task. *Journal of Environmental Psychology,* 2(1): 3–22.

Groat, Linda N. 1984. Public opinions of contextual fit. *Architecture,* 73(11): 72–75.

Groat, Linda N. 1988. Contextual compatibility in architecture: An issue of personal tastes? In *Environmental Aesthetics: Theory, Research and Application,* ed. Jack L. Nasar, pp. 228–53. New York: Cambridge University Press.

Habraken, John. 1972. *Supports: An Alternative to Mass Housing.* Cambridge: MIT Press.

Hall, Edward T. 1963. A system for the notation of proxemic behavior. *American Anthropologist.* 65: 1003–1026.

Hall, Edward T. 1966. *The Hidden Dimension.* Garden City, NY: Doubleday.

Halprin, Lawrence. 1965. Motation. *Progressive Architecture.* 46(7): 126–133.

Halprin, Lawrence. 1969. *The RSVP Cycles: Creative Processes in the Human Environment.* New York: Braziller.

Halprin, Lawrence, and James Burns. 1974. *Taking Part: A Workshop Approach to Collective Creativity.* Cambridge: MIT Press.

Hart, Roger, and Gary T. Moore. 1973. The development of spatial cognition. A review. In *Image and Environment: Cognitive Mapping and Spatial Behavior,* eds. Roger M. Downs and David Stea, pp. 246–88. Chicago: Aldine.

Hebb, Donald O. 1949. *The Organization of Behavior.* New York: Wiley.

Heimsath, Clovis, and Ben Heimsath. 1989. Computerizing behavioral design. *Architecture,* 78(6): 154–56.

Hershberger, Robert G., and Robert C. Cass. 1974. Predicting user responses to buildings. In *Field Applications,* ed. Gerald Davis, pp. 117–134. *EDRA-5: Evaluation and Applications,* ed. Dan Carson. Washington, DC: Environmental Design Research Association.

Hochberg, Julian. 1966. Representative sampling and the purposes of research. In *The Psychology of Egon Brunswik,* ed. Kenneth Hammond, pp. 361–381. Fort Worth, TX: Holt, Rinehart and Winston.

Hochberg, Julian. 1978. *Perception: Second Edition:* Englewood Cliffs, NJ: Prentice Hall.

Hochberg, Julian, and V. Brooks. 1978. Psychological aspects of the cinema. In *Handbook of Perception,* Vol X. eds. Edward C. Carterette and M.P. Friedman. New York: Academic Press.

Howard, Roger B., T. Gervan Mlynarski, and Gordon C. Sauer, Jr. 1972. A comparative analysis of affective responses to real and represented environments. In *Environmental Design: Research and Practice,* Proceedings of the Third Environmental Design Research Association Conference, ed. William J. Mitchell, pp. 6-6-1 to 6-6-8. Los Angeles: UCLA.

Huberlein, Thomas A., and Peter Dunwiddie. 1979. Systematic observation of use levels, campsite selection and visitor characteristics at a high mountain lake. *Journal of Leisure Research,* 11: 307–16.

Hunt, Michael E. 1985. Enhancing a building's imageability. *Journal of Architectural and Planning Research,* 2: 151–168.

Irving, Robert 1985. *History and Design of the Australian House.* Melbourne: Oxford University Press.

Ittleson, William H. 1960. *Visual Space Perception.* New York: Springer.

Ittleson, William, Harold M. Proshansky, and Leanne G. Rivlin. 1970. Freedom of choice and behavior in a physical setting. In *Environmental Psychology: Man and His Physical Setting,* eds. Harold M. Proshansky, William Ittleson, and Leanne G. Rivlin, pp. 173–82. Fort Worth, TX: Holt, Rinehart and Winston.

Jacobs, Glenn. 1970. *The Participant Observer.* New York: Braziller.

Janssens, Jan, and Rikard R. Küller. 1986. Utilizing an environmental simulation laboratory in Sweden. In *Foundations for Visual Analysis,* eds. Richard C. Smardon, James F. Palmer, and John P. Felleman, pp. 265–275. New York: Wiley.

Jensen, Luther. 1952. Measuring family solidarity. *American Sociological Review,* 17: 727–33.

Jones, Christopher. 1970. *Design Methods.* New York: Wiley.

Kaplan, Stephen. 1973. Cognitive maps, human needs and the designed environment. In *Environmental Design Research, Volume 1,* ed. Wolfgang F. E. Preiser, pp. 275–83. Stroudsburg, PA: Dowden, Hutchinson, & Ross.

Kaplan, Stephen. 1977. Participation in the design process: A cognitive approach. In *Perspectives on Environment and Behavior,* ed. Daniel Stokols, pp. 221–23. New York: Plenum.

Kaplan, Stephen. 1979. Perception and landscape: Conceptions and misconceptions. In *Our National Landscape,* eds. Gary H. Elsner and Richard C. Smardon, pp. 241–48. USDA Forest Service, General Technical Report, PSW-35. Berkeley.

Kaplan, Stephen, and Rachel R. Kaplan. 1982. *Cognition and Environment: Functioning in an Uncertain World*. New York: Praeger.

Kasmar, Joyce V. 1988. The development of a usable lexicon of environmental description. *Environmental Aesthetics: Theory, Research and Applications*, ed. Jack L. Nasar, pp. 144–55. New York: Cambridge University Press.

Kelly, George A. 1955. *The Psychology of Personal Constructs*. New York: W. W. Norton.

Krampen, Martin. 1979. *Meaning in the Urban Environment*. London: Pion Limited.

Lawrence, Roderick J. 1981. The optimization of habitat: The user's approach to design. *Open House*, 6(3): 35–44.

Leff, Herbert. 1984. *Playful Perception: Choosing How to Express Your World*. Burlington, VT: Waterfront.

Lewin, Kurt. 1946. Action research and minority problems. *Journal of Social Issues*, 2: 34–36.

Litton, Robert B. 1968. *Forest Landscape Description and Inventories*. USDA Forest Service, Research Paper PSW-49, Berkeley, CA.

Low, Jim. 1980. Adelaide Road: Tenant participation. *Architects Journal*, 171(9): 432–437.

Low, Setha M., and William P. Ryan 1985. Noticing without looking: A methodology for the integration of architectural and local perceptions in Oley, Pennsylvania. *Journal of Architectural and Planning Research*, 2: 3–22.

Lowenthal, David, and Marquita Riel. 1972. The nature of perceived and imagined environments. *Environment and Behavior*, 4(2): 189–207.

Lozano, Eduardo E. 1988. Visual needs in urban environments and physical planning. In *Environmental Aesthetics: Theory, Research and Applications*, ed. Jack L. Nasar, pp. 395–421. New York: Cambridge University Press.

Lynch, Kevin. 1960. *Image of the City*. Cambridge: MIT Press.

Lynch, Kevin. 1977(a). *Growing Up In Cities: Studies in the Spatial Environment of Adolescence in Cracow, Melbourne, Mexico City, Salta, Toluca, and Warszawa*. Cambridge: MIT Press.

Lynch, Kevin. 1977(b). *Managing the Sense of a Region*. Cambridge: MIT Press.

Lynch, Kevin, and Malcolm Rivkin. 1970. A walk around the block. *In Environmental Psychology: Man and his Physical Setting*, eds. Harold M. Proshansky, William H. Ittelson, and Leanne G. Rivlin, pp. 631–641. Fort Worth, TX: Holt, Rinehart and Winston.

Marcus, Claire Cooper, and Wendy Sarkissian. 1986. *Housing as if People Mattered: Site Design Guidelines for Medium-Density Family Housing*. Berkeley: University of California Press.

Mainardi-Peron, Erminielda, Maria R. Baroni, Remo Job, and Paola Salmaso. 1985. Cognitive factors and communicative strategies in recalling unfamiliar places. *Journal of Environmental Psychology*, 5: 325–333.

Matti, Hans and Peter Von Meiss. 1982. *The LEA*, Laboratoire d'experimentation architecturale Newsletter 2. Ecole Polytechnique Federale, Lausanne.

McKechnie, George E. 1974. *Manual for the Environmental Response Inventory*. Palo Alto, CA: Consulting Psychologists Press.

Metzger, John. 1989. Visual solutions: Exploring a new design ethic. *Microcad News*, 4(2): 37–38.

Miller, George A., Eugene Galanter, and Karl H. Pribram. 1960. *Plans and the Structure of Behavior*. New York: Holt.

Mitchell, William. 1977. *Computer Aided Architectural Design*. New York: Petrocelli/Charter.

Moore, Charles. 1984. Working to make something. *Architectural Record*, 172: 94–103.

Moore, Gary T., and Reginald G. Golledge. 1976. *Environmental Knowing*. Stroudsburg, PA: Dowden, Hutchinson & Ross.

Moore, Robin C. 1986. The power of nature orientations of girls and boys toward biotic and abiotic play settings on a reconstructed schoolyard. *Children's Environments Quarterly*, 3(3): 52–69.

Nasar, Jack L. 1988. Perception and evaluation of residential street scenes. In *Environmental Aesthetics: Theory, Research, and Applications*, ed. Jack L. Nasar, pp. 275–89. New York: Cambridge University Press.

Nasar, Jack L. 1989. Symbolic meaning of house styles. *Environment and Behavior*, 21(3): 235–257.

Neeley, Dennis. 1989. Animation in architecture. *Cadence*, 4(4): 37–9.

Neisser, Ulrich. 1976. *Cognition and Reality*. San Francisco: Freeman.

Nelson, Doreen G. 1974. *Manual for the City Building Education Program*. Washington, DC: National Endowment for the Arts.

Newman, Oscar. 1972. *Defensible Space: Crime Prevention through Urban Design*. New York: Macmillan.

Oakley, R. 1980. *Profiles and perspectives of hostel residents*. MSc. dissertation, University of Surrey.

Oberdorfer, Jeff. 1988. Community participation in the design of the Boulder Creek library. *Design Studies* 9(1): 4–13.

O'Keefe, John, and Lynn Nadel. 1978. *The Hoppocampus as a Cognitive Map*. Oxford: Oxford University Press.

Olver, Rose R., and Joan R. Hornsby. 1966. On equivalence. In *Studies in Cognitive Growth,* eds. Jerome S. Bruner, Rose R. Olver, and Patricia M. Greenfield, pp. 68–85. New York: Wiley.

Osgood, Charles E., George Suci, and Percy H. Tannenbaum. 1957. *The Measurement of Meaning.* Urbana, IL: University of Illinois Press.

Osmond, Humphrey. 1959. The relationship between architect and psychiatrist. In *Psychiatric Architecture,* ed. Charles Goshen, Washington: American Psychiatric Association.

Ostrander, Edward. 1974. The visual-semantic communication gap: A model and some implications for collaboration between architects and behavioral scientists. *Man Environment Systems,* 4.1: 47–53.

Palmer, James E. 1986. Environmental perception. In *Foundations for Visual Project Analysis,* eds. Richard C. Smardon, James E. Palmer, and John P. Felleman, pp. 64–77. New York: Wiley.

Parr, Albert E. 1966. Psychological aspects of urbanology, *Journal of Social Issues,* 22: 40.

Passini, Romedi. 1984. *Wayfinding in Architecture.* New York: Van Nostrand Reinhold.

Pearlman, Kenneth T. 1988. Aesthetic regulation and the courts. In *Environmental Aesthetics: Theory, Research, and Applications,* ed. Jack Nasar, pp. 476–492. New York: Cambridge University Press.

Pitt, David G., and Ervin H. Zube. 1979. The Q-sort method: Use in landscape assessment research and landscape planning. In *Our National Landscape,* eds. Gary H. Elsner and Richard C. Smardon, pp. 227–34. USDA Forest Service, General Technical Report, PSW-35, Berkeley.

Pfaffman, Carl. 1960. The pleasures of sensation. *Psychology Review* 67: 253–268.

Pratt, Joanne H., James Pratt, Sarah B. Moore, and William T. Moore. 1979. *Environmental Encounter: Experiences in Decision Making for the Built and Natural Environment.* Dallas, TX: Reverchon.

Proshansky, Harold, and Bernard Seidenberg. 1965. *Basic Studies in Social Psychology.* Fort Worth, TX: Holt, Rinehart and Winston.

Purcell, A. Terry, J. Robert Metcalfe, Ross Thorne, and Rob Hall. 1972. *Office Environments: Comparison of User Responses to Two Clerical Office Spaces of different layouts in the One Organization and Building.* Sydney, Australia: I. B. Fell Research Center, University of Sydney.

Purcell, A. Terry. 1986. Environmental perception and affect: A schema discrepancy model. *Environment and Behavior,* 18: 3–30.

Rapoport, Amos. 1960. *House Form and Culture.* Englewood Cliffs, NJ: Prentice Hall.

Rapoport, Amos. 1971. Some observations regarding man-environment studies. *Art,* 2: 1.

Rapoport, Amos. 1977. *Human Aspects of Urban Form.* New York: Pergamon.

Rapoport, Amos. 1982. *The Meaning of the Built Environment.* Beverly Hills, CA: Sage Publications.

Rapoport, Amos, and Robert E. Kantor. 1967. Complexity and ambiguity in environmental design. *Journal of the American Institute of Planners,* 33: 210–221.

Robertson, Edward G. 1979. *Carlton.* Melbourne: Ribgy Limited.

Saarinen, Tom F. 1976. *Environmental Planning: Perception and Behavior.* Boston: Houghton Mifflin.

Sanoff, Henry. 1970a. House form and preference. In *EDRA Two: Proceedings of the Second Annual Environmental Design Research Association Conference,* eds. John Archea and Charles Eastman, pp. 334–339. Pittsburgh, PA: Carnegie Mellon University.

Sanoff, Henry. 1970b. *Social Perception of the Neighborhood.* Raleigh: North Carolina State University, School of Design.

Sanoff, Henry. 1973. Youth's perception and categorizations of residential cues. In *Environmental Design Research,* Volume 1, ed. Wolfgang F. E. Preiser, pp. 84–97. Stroudsburg, PA: Dowden, Hutchinson and Ross.

Sanoff, Henry. 1974a. Systematic evaluation of architectural requirements for community housing. *Designing the Method,* ed. David Tester, pp. 245–55. Raleigh: North Carolina State University. Volume 23.

Sanoff, Henry. 1974b. Measuring attributes of the visual environment. In *Designing for Human Behavior,* eds. Jon Lang, Charles Burnett, Walter Moleski, and David Vachon. pp. 244–60. New York: Van Nostrand Reinhold.

Sanoff, Henry. 1979. *Designing with Community Participation.* New York: Van Nostrand Reinhold.

Sanoff, Henry. 1982. *Planning Outdoor Play.* Atlanta, GA: Humanics.

Sanoff, Henry. 1983. *Arts Center Workbook.* Raleigh, NC: North Carolina State University, School of Design. (Team participants included Marilia DoVal, Sergio Ortiz, Chainarong Ratanacharoensiri, and Li-Shan Lee.)

Sanoff, Henry. 1988. Community arts facilities. *Design Studies,* 9(1): 25–39.

Sanoff, Henry. 1988. Residential infill: A fabric design strategy. *Architecture Australia,* 77(1): 36–39.

Sanoff, Henry, and Gary J. Coates. 1971. Behavior mapping. *International Journal of Environmental Studies.* 2: 234.

Sanoff, Henry and George Barbour, 1974. An Alternative Strategy for Planning an Alternative School. In *Alternative Learning Environments*, ed. Gary J. Coates, pp. 157–169. Stroudsburgh, PA: Dowden, Hutchinson and Ross.

Sanoff, Henry, Greg Centeno, and Susan Goltsman. 1976. *Asheville Environmental Workbook*. Raleigh, NC: North Carolina State University, School of Design, Community Development Group.

Sanoff, Henry, Graham Adams, Kay Brasaunas, and Theresa Hawkins. 1977. *Planning with People: Designing a Campsite*. Raleigh: NC State University, School of Design, Community Development Group.

Seaton, Richard, and John Collins. 1972. Validity and reliability of ratings of simulated buildings. In *Environmental Design: Research and Practice*, Proceedings of the Third Environmental Design Research Association Conference, ed. William J. Mitchell, pp. 6–10–1 to 6–10–12. Los Angeles: UCLA.

Shafer, Ellwood L., Jr. 1969. Perception of natural environments. *Environment and Behavior*, 1: 71–82.

Sheppard, Stephen R. J. 1988. How credible are visual simulations? *Landscape Architecture*, 73(1): 83–84.

Sheppard, Stephen R. J. 1988. Simulating changes in the landscape. In *Foundations for Visual Project Analysis*, eds. Richard C. Smardon, James F. Palmer, and John P. Felleman, pp. 187–99. New York: Wiley.

Sheppard, Stephen R. J. 1989. *Visual Simulation: A User's Guide for Architects, Engineers, and Planners*. New York: Van Nostrand Reinhold.

Sherif, Muzafer, and Carol W. Sherif. 1963. Varieties of social stimulus situations. In *Stimulus Determinants of Behavior*, ed Saul B. Sells, pp. 82–106. New York: Ronald.

Sloan, Sam. 1970. *Clerks are People*. Sydney, Australia: University of Sydney, School of Architecture.

Southworth, Michael. 1969. The sonic environment of cities. *Journal of Environment and Behavior*, 1(1): 49–70.

Stea, David. 1965. Space, territory, and human movement, *Landscape* 15: 13–16.

Stea, David. 1969. Environmental perception and cognition: Toward a model for mental maps. In *Response to Environment*, eds. Gary J. Coates and Kenneth M. Moffett, pp. 63–76. Raleigh: North Carolina State University. Vol. 18.

Steinitz, Victoria. 1971. *How Children Categorize Social Stimuli*. Washington, DC: Department of Health, Education & Welfare, National Center for Education Research.

Studer, Ray and David Stea. 1967. *Directory of Behavior and Environmental Design.* Providence, Rhode Island: Research and Design Institute of Providence.

Suttles Gerald. 1972. *The Social Construction of Communities.* Chicago: University of Chicago Press.

Taylor, Jonathan G., Ervin H. Zube, and James L. Sell. 1987. Landscape assessment and perception research methods. In *Methods in Environmental and Behavioral Research,* eds. Robert B. Bechtel, Robert W. Marans, and William Michelson, pp. 161–193. New York: Van Nostrand Reinhold.

Thiel, Philip. 1961. A sequence-experience notation for architectural and urban spaces. *Town Planning Review,* 32(1): 33–52.

Thiel, Philip, Ean D. Harrison, and Richard S. Alden. 1986. The Perception of Spatial Enclosure as a Function of the Position of Architectural Surfaces. *Environment and Behavior,* 18(2): 227–245.

Turner, Charles. 1978. Yerba Buena Planning Ballot. In *Designing with Community Participation,* ed. Henry Sanoff, pp. 205–7. New York: Van Nostrand Reinhold.

United States Forest Service. 1973. *National Forest Landscape Management.* Vol. 1. U.S. Department of Agriculture, Agriculture Handbook no. 434, Washington, DC: US Government Printing Office.

Vasilopoulos, A. 1988. Creating Precision Graphics. *Computer Graphics World.* December.

Vigier, Francois. 1965. An experimental approach to urban design. *Journal of the American Institute of Planners* 31(2): 21–29.

Wagner, Jon. 1979. Perceiving a planned community. In *Images of Information,* ed. Jon Wagner, pp. 85–101. Beverly Hills, CA: Sage Publications.

Wagner, Philip L. 1972. Cultural landscapes and regions: Aspects of communication. In *Man, Space and Environment,* eds. Paul W. English and Robert C. Mayfield, pp. 55–68. New York: Oxford.

Walker, Rob, and Janine Wiedel. 1985. Using photographs in a discipline of words. In *Field Methods in the Study of Education,* ed. Robert G. Burgess, pp.191–216. London: The Falmer Press.

Ward, Colin and Anthony Fryson. 1973. *Streetwork-the Exploding School.* London: Routledge and Kegan Paul.

Ward, Lawrence M., and James A. Russell. 1981. Cognitive set and the perception of place. *Environment and Behavior,* 13(5): 610–632.

Webb, Eugene J., Donald T. Campbell, Richard D. Schwartz, and Lee L. Seechrest. 1972. *Unobtrusive Measures: Nonreactive Research in the Social Sciences.* Chicago: Rand McNally. pp. 116–17.

Weiss, Robert S., and Serge Boutourline, Jr. 1962. *Fairs, Exhibits, Pavilions and Their Audiences.* New York: IBM Corporation.

Welsh, W. Thomas. 1988. Profile of an architect. *Cadence,* 3.11: 52–56.

Wener, Richard. 1989. Post occupancy evaluation. In *Advances in Evaluation of the Built Environment,* eds. Ervin H. Zube and Gary T. Moore, pp. 287–310. New York: Plenum.

Wheeler, Kenneth. 1976. Experiencing townscape. *Bulletin of Environmental Education.* 68: 11–13.

Winders, R., and L. S. Gray. 1973. *The Urban Trail.* Sheffield, England: Pavic Productions.

Winkel, Gary, and Robert Sasanoff. 1966. *An Approach to an Objective Analysis of Behavior in Architectural Space.* Architectural Development Series no. 5, Seattle: University of Washington, Department of Architecture.

Winkel, Gary, Roger Malek, and Philip Thiel. 1970. A study of human responses to selected roadside environments. *EDRA-1,* eds. Henry Sanoff and Sidney Cohn. DHR Research Association.

Wohlwill, Joachim F. 1976. Environmental aesthetics: The environment as a source of affect. In *Human Behavior and Environment, Volume 1,* eds. Irwin Altman and Joachim F. Wohlwill, pp. 37–86. New York: Plenum.

Young, Michael, and Peter Willmott. 1957. *Family and Kinship in East London.* London: Kegan Paul.

Zube, Ervin H. 1973. Rating everyday landscapes of the northeastern United States. *Landscape Architecture,* 63(3): 370–375.

Zube, Ervin H. 1976. *Perceiving Environmental Quality: Research and Applications.* New York: Plenum.

Zube, Ervin H., David G. Pitt, and Thomas W. Anderson. 1974. *Perception and Measurement of Scenic Resource Values in the Southern Connecticut River Valley.* Univ. of Massachusetts, Institute of Man and Environment, Publication no. R-74-1. Amherst.

Zube, Ervin H., Julius G. Fabos, and Robert O. Brush. 1975. *Landscape Assessment.* Stroudsburg, PA: Dowden, Hutchinson and Ross.

Index